CASES IN MARKETING MANAGEMENT AND STRATEGY

VOLUME 2

Edited by
Gerry Mortimer

The Marketing Institute

Print origination by Artwerk
Printed in Ireland by ColourBooks Ltd.

ISBN 0 9529076 4 X

CONTENTS

ABOUT THE CONTRIBUTORS

EDEL FOLEY lectures in marketing and management at the Dublin Institute of Technology, Mountjoy Square. She has written several well-known books and articles on the subjects of marketing and management, and is the author of *The Irish Market - A Profile* for The Marketing Institute.

TONY GALLAGHER is Professor of Education and Assistant Director and Head of Research Division of the Graduate School of Education at the Queen's University of Belfast. His research interests include the role of education in ethnically divided societies, education for social inclusion and access and participation in higher education.

TRISH MEDCALF is a lecturer in marketing and management at the Institute of Technology, Tallaght. She has been involved in a number of research and consultancy projects in the Tallaght region. She joined the Institute in 1997 having worked with a corporate identity consultancy as well as in industrial and direct marketing.

JOHN MILLIKEN lectures in marketing and distribution management at the University of Ulster. His research interests include educational management and strategic supply chain management. Prior to commencing an academic career, he held a number of senior posts in strategic management within the food industry.

GERRY MORTIMER is a lecturer in Marketing at the DIT Faculty of Business. He is the author of several case studies and also works extensively as a consultant to Irish industry and development agencies.

MICHAEL MURPHY joined the Department of Management & Marketing in UCC in 1997. He lectures in market research and business-to-business Marketing. Prior to starting in UCC he worked for almost three years with BMR Ltd, an Irish-owned company which manufactures and markets the Slendertone range of products. Michael is currently pursuing his doctoral studies in the area of e-commerce.

DON O'SULLIVAN is a lecturer in marketing at UCC. His research interests are the interface between marketing and organization climate and Internet marketing.

JOHN O'SULLIVAN is with ACT Venture Capital. He has a particular interest in the strategic and marketing issues faced by hi-tech Irish start-up companies.

ANN M TORRES lectures in the NUI Galway in promotion management, marketing management and business-to-business marketing. Prior to coming to Galway, she studied for her MBA at University of California at Berkeley. Her research interests are entrepreneurship and ethics.

MARY WILCOX is a lecturer in the School of Retail and Services Management, Faculty of Business, Dublin Institute of Technology. Her subject areas are consumer behaviour, communications and personal development; particular interests include retail strategy and case writing.

PREFACE

This is the fourth volume of case studies in this series. The project was conceived at the Irish Marketing Teachers Association (IMTA) conference in Galway in 1992. The first competition took place in 1993 and it has since become a biennial event with the best of the cases being published in the year following each competition. The Marketing Institute has been the enthusiastic sponsor since the inception of the competition and has published or funded the publishing of each volume to date as well as providing a substantial prize fund for winning cases. The competition has been of value both to The Marketing Institute, which uses many of the cases on its Graduateship programme, and to the marketing teaching community. The cases are widely used on case study programmes in Irish universities and institutes of technology. In all, thirty cases have been published as a result of this competition.

Some new case writers emerged from the 1999 competition. It was also heartening to see some previous contributors returning. There was a good balance of cases between small business and large corporation with the new and emerging technologies also well represented.

A major change in the competition on this occasion was the retiring of two of the judges, Jim Ward and Tony Cunningham. Jim, Professor of Marketing in NUI Galway, is now Vice President there, while Tony has, nominally, retired from his position as Professor of Marketing in UCD. The word *nominally* is used, as Tony remains as active as ever. Both IMTA and The Marketing Institute are heavily indebted to Jim and Tony for their contribution to the development of the competition. This writer and Dr Brenda Cullen of UCD have joined Catherine KilBride, Director-Education, The Marketing Institute, as judges of this fourth competition. Both the new judges are previous contributors to the competition. From this writer's experience, it is perhaps easier to be a contributor than a judge.

In passing, it should be noted that the judges were somewhat disappointed with the number of case studies entered for the competition. This reached a peak in 1997 in the third competition but has fallen back somewhat in this instance. To make this volume comparable in scale to previous volumes, two further cases developed by this writer were added. These cases were used in The Marketing Institute Graduate Entry Case Study Examination which takes place in November every year. Waterford Crystal was used in 1997 and National Irish Bank in 1998.

As in previous volumes, it is useful to examine the criteria used in assessing cases for this competition. These are criteria which those of us who teach case study programmes well recognise. The criteria developed and refined by the judges of the earlier competitions stand the test of time well and were again used in this competition. They have been slightly adapted for use in this preface.

Some elaboration on the criteria may be of value.

1. Structure, Presentation and Narrative

A good case study is first of all a story. It is, however, a story with a purpose. It will draw the student into areas of both analysis and prescription. It therefore has to be well introduced. An opening paragraph setting up the case is of some importance. A good flow which brings the reader along is also a major benefit.

2. Case Focus/Issues

Case studies can operate at many different levels and achieve many different results across a wide range of disciplines. As a teacher of marketing case study programmes which typically use up to 16/18 at final year undergraduate and postgraduate level, this writer is constantly seeking new case studies to rejuvenate a programme, replace cases that are 'past their sell by date' or for use in an examination. A good case study demands your immediate attention. It is of immense benefit to have an opening paragraph which sets up the focus and issues to be examined. In this context a case study is to be distinguished from a case history. Both have their roles to play in education. In this writer's opinion, case histories function most usefully at the two extreme ends of business education. At the basic level, a good case history can provide the student with clear examples to illustrate a point in a lecture or text. At the other end of the spectrum, in programmes for practising managers, it can provide a fruitful base for a group discussion. Peters and Waterman's tome, *In Search of Excellence,* is perhaps the best known example of this genre in the last two decades. On the other hand a key attribute for a good case study is that it can function at several levels, and give value at all or most of them.

A good case study lends itself to:
- the individual examination by a student working on his or her own
- the subsequent drawing together of different views in a group discussion where both analysis and prescription can be developed
- a well structured presentation to a peer group and/or a facilitator
- wider class discussion and the drawing out of learnings by a facilitator.

To function at these different levels, a case study must strike a balance between material for analysis and the opportunity for the student to take the case forward. A good case study is therefore rich in issues, balancing the definition of the problem with the need to allow students to discover and develop issues for themselves. A good teaching note can show the case author's view of what the issues are and also indicates the level for which the case is suitable.

3. Opportunities to demonstrate marketing principles and apply marketing techniques
In addition to showing a student's ability to handle complex issues, a case study programme also provides an opportunity to assess a student's ability to demonstrate an understanding of marketing principles and of the various models and techniques which have been developed. These will have been at the core of earlier programmes undertaken by students now pursuing a case study programme. Case studies which facilitate such use of principles and techniques assist both student and teacher.

4. Decision-Making

As previously noted, a major role of a case study is to look forward and to direct the student towards decision-making. A key element in decision-making is the examination of options. A good case study will create different options and allow for different bundling of options into a decision-making framework. It is a bonus if a case study offers opportunities for students to be creative in their thinking and, in particular, to think "outside the dots."

5. Relevance to Current Issues

All case studies have a shelf life. An issue or situation which today seems of vital importance may, tomorrow, be overtaken by events. The Aer Rianta case in this volume illustrates this. It is set just prior to the abolition of duty free, at the end of a lengthy rear guard action to preserve it. Though the case study offers a rich quota of issues, it is clear that duty free will gradually fade from the scene. It can be a difficult balance to strike. Cases which address current issues in marketing practice and which reflect developments in the environment in which decision-making must take place are invaluable.

6. Teaching Notes

The competition requires the provision of a teaching note to accompany the case study. This writer has always had a somewhat ambivalent view on case teaching notes. As a case writer, it is an excellent discipline to develop a usable teaching note for others who might use the case study. It is also a chore, typically undertaken in response to some deadline or request long after the case study is complete. As a case teacher, this writer has found a teaching note, even a well developed one, of limited value, and only refers to the case teaching note to discover what happened next. Perhaps it might best be described as a necessary evil! The European Case Clearing House (ECCH) do not require a teaching note to be submitted when registering a case study but they do have clear guidelines for teaching notes which they publish.

These are:
• Summary of the case

- Teaching objectives and target audience
- Teaching approach and strategy
- Analysis and techniques recommended
- Additional readings and references if necessary or helpful
- Feedback on use or suitability and/or update on the case situation.

One issue which this writer had not come across before in assessing teaching notes arose in this competition. In this instance, the case writer introduced significant new material in the teaching note which should have either been excluded or included in the case study.

Finally, before discussing the winners, a few brief general points might be added. Case studies should be properly proof read, sources of data should be referenced and text should be clear and well presented. As Jim Ward noted in editing the previous volume, if one is putting a case study into the public domain, it should be marketed! For those interested in furthering their work in this area, the ECCH is of considerable assistance. Jim Erskine and Mike Leenders of the University of Western Ontario have written a number of texts on case writing and teaching. These are published by the university. The World Association of Case Research and Application (WACRA) holds an annual conference at the end of June or early July. In 2000 it will be in Budapest and in 2001 in Sweden. WACRA's web site is www.wacra.org.

THE WINNERS

The adjudicators were unanimous in their view that the outstanding case was *Marketing and Growth Strategies : A Software Case,* developed by Don O'Sullivan of UCC and John O'Sullivan of ACT Venture Capital. This case raises several interesting and current issues in software marketing on a global basis to complex purchasing organisations. The case is presented at a critical stage in the company's development and is rich in options that can be considered by the directors and their advisors. The accompanying teaching note addresses these issues comprehensively.

The selection of other awards was a more difficult task with several of the cases of a similar standard. After much discussion, the runner-up awards went to Edel Foley of DIT for *Blooming Clothing: The Case for Renewal,* and to Ann Torres of NUI Galway for *Judy Greene Pottery: Marketing Irish Handcrafted Products.* Ann has been a consistent supporter of the competition and a prize winner previously.

OVERVIEW OF CASES

MARKETING & GROWTH STRATEGIES
– A SOFTWARE CASE
DON O'SULLIVAN & JOHN O'SULLIVAN

Qumas is an indigenous Irish software company which has developed rapidly over a period of five years, through identifying a particular niche which appears to offer good prospects of success. At the point at which the case is written, it faces major challenges and must reflect carefully on how it should meet those marketing challenges.

BLOOMING CLOTHING : THE CASE FOR RENEWAL
EDEL FOLEY

This case study looks at an Irish SME operating in a definable niche market - maternity wear - in the highly mature and competitive clothing industry. The company has successfully established itself against formidable competition in both retail and manufacturing. How Blooming moves forward in a changing environment is at the heart of this case study.

JUDY GREENE POTTERY : MARKETING IRISH
HANDCRAFTED PRODUCTS
ANN M. TORRES

Most handcraft companies do not develop beyond mircrobusiness scale either because the market does not justify development, or for lifestyle reasons. This case looks at a company which has developed to a stage where it is competing with the other major players in its sector. The story of its development is an interesting one but it also presents strategic options for the company's future and is supported by comprehensive visual material.

RETAILING AT DUBLIN AIRPORT – A GROWTH
STRATEGY FOR THE NEW MILLENNIUM
MARY WILCOX

Few businesses face a change in their environment as fundamental as that facing Aer Rianta as duty free is about to be abolished, despite a strong rearguard action by vested interests including Aer Rianta and the Irish Government. How to cope with, and respond to, such change is the principal focus of this case.

REPOSITIONING EIRCELL AND BUILDING A VALUABLE BRAND
PATRICIA MEDCALF

This case study examines Eircell at a key point in its development as it faces towards a more competitive and rapidly growing market. In particular, it examines the current and future branding strategy for the product.

SLENDERTONE : CREATING A WORLD CLASS BRAND
MICHAEL MURPHY

The Slendertone case examines the development of a highly successful consumer product which came from humble beginnings. The case study provides excellent material for examining how the company achieved its market position and the obstacles which were placed in its way. The company has ambitions to become a world class brand. The case also examines how this might be achieved.

STRATEGIC MARKETING FOR EDUCATION IN A DIVIDED SOCIETY
JOHN MILLIKEN AND TONY GALLAGHER

This case examines the market for integrated education in Northern Ireland against the background of the civil conflict there. It provides considerable primary and secondary research data for analysis.

As noted previously, two further case studies have been added to this volume, both by Gerry Mortimer. These case studies were used in the Marketing Institute Graduate Entry Case Study examination in 1997 and 1998. This examination provides an accelerated route to Graduate Membership of the Institute for marketing graduates from the universities and institutes of technology.

WATERFORD CRYSTAL, THE CHAIRMAN'S CHALLENGE
GERRY MORTIMER

This case deals with one of Ireland's few truly international brands. It is set in 1995 when the company has successfully completed a recovery programme and is looking forward to a period of growth. This growth has been encapsulated in a target to which the incoming Chief Executive has signed up – that of doubling turnover and profit within five years. How such a target might be achieved is the principal focus of this case.

NATIONAL IRISH BANK : COPING WITH A CRISIS AND BEYOND
GERRY MORTIMER

Early in 1998, National Irish Bank, a relatively small player in the Irish market, was faced with a series of crises as media became aware of problems in the bank. This case study examines the nature of these problems and invites students to suggest how the bank might respond to its problems and how it might look to develop in the longer term, given its parent company objectives.

Gerry Mortimer
DIT-Faculty of Business

MARKETING AND GROWTH STRATEGIES - A SOFTWARE CASE

Don O'Sullivan and John O'Sullivan

INTRODUCTION

Paul Hands had just closed up shop for Christmas and Qumas, the company he founded four years earlier, was in good shape. That day's edition of The Irish Times had described Qumas as one of the "rising stars" in the rapidly emerging Irish information technology sector. There had been quite a buzz within Qumas for the previous six months as they started to win significant business in Europe and the United States. They had recently increased the number of employees to thirty and there were plans to add further to this. But Paul took most satisfaction from the fact that competitors were starting to take notice of Qumas and to bench-mark against them on a regular basis.

Qumas produced and marketed document management software. This type of software was used by large companies to increase the quality / efficiency and decrease the time / cost associated with managing complex documents in business units and more recently across their organizations. Qumas was in a very attractive market, with cash rich customers looking for products that could make a real difference to their overall performance. Best of all, Qumas was in a market that had been more than doubling in size each year since 1995.

Paul worried that this growth might affect Qumas's market niche and relative competitive advantage. Competitors were consolidating and customers were becoming even more exacting. These issues would be top of the next board meeting agenda in January. Over the Christmas holidays, Paul planned to spend some time analyzing the options with David Grimes, Donal Olden and Kevin O'Leary, the company's cofounders. Qumas's market position and success allowed choices; the challenge now was to choose and implement a marketing strategy that would leverage their success and capitalize on the market changes.

COMPANY BACKGROUND

The origins of the Qumas product began in 1994. The founders were running a company called QCL, supplying computer hardware and services to local companies in the Irish market. QCL was enjoying steady performance. Because of the concentration of the pharmaceutical industry in Ireland and particularly in the Southern region, QCL had a significant client base from the sector.

Over time, relationships with these clients deepened and QCL became increasingly involved with their business. In particular, QCL became aware of the problems associated with regulatory compliance (certain industries, such as pharmaceuticals, are subject to strict regulatory control from bodies like the Food and Drug Administration (FDA) in the U.S). These problems concerned the time and cost of maintaining large amounts of documented information relating to quality control, production processes etc.

The FDA operates internationally, and is entitled to visit any location where a product licensed for sale in the U.S. is manufactured. Its standard setting process leads that of other national regulatory bodies. The FDA must see evidence that the company has controls in place and how these have operated over time. A key element of the inspection process is a review of the documentation that describes what the company makes and how. QCL was asked by several of its customers to work with them to solve these problems. This work became the starting point for the development of the Qumas product.

Integrated Document Management (IDM) technology was being employed to solve this problem and deliver benefits on two fronts. Firstly, to speed new product release by providing speedier creation of product-related documentation. Secondly, to protect companies in the case of audits carried out by the FDA.

Keeping the master copy up to date is difficult enough, but keeping copies of this, which are distributed around the plant, under control is an even greater headache. Such issues can make regulated document control very difficult. This gloomy picture, which regards the control of company procedures as a hindrance rather than an aid, is all too familiar among regulated companies.

Howmedica (Limerick) and FMC (Cork) provided QCL with an opportunity to "productize" their solution and gave the company initial confidence in the wider market potential. As a result of this, a new and separate company was formed - Qumas. Essentially, Qumas's goal was to provide a software product which addressed document management problems for companies operating within these regulated environments.

Significantly, Ireland represents a microcosm of the global pharmaceutical industry, with many leading companies having production sites in the region. Consequently, success in Ireland provided good references for accessing international markets. Working with the local sites of these multinationals provided an opportunity for Qumas to prove itself, refine the product, generate turnover and develop contacts at HQ levels within these client companies.

Through 1995, Qumas carried out extensive market and product research, both domestically and abroad. They spoke with many industry specialists and regulatory bodies. Software prototypes were used to gather industry opinions and Qumas then formulated a detailed system specification. The management team secured a £1million investment in venture capital and a further £500,000 from Enterprise Ireland to finance product and market development. In late 1995, the first version of Qumas was released to the market[1].

THE ROLE OF THE FOOD AND DRUG ADMINISTRATION (FDA)

The role of the FDA in regulation is crucial; it ensures the safety of the public through the licensing of companies' products. With rigorous enforcement through testing and audits, it is the FDA that decides who can produce the products. Every organization that compiles procedure documents knows that gaining acceptance by regulatory bodies such as the FDA, is only the first step. The initial elation of achieving certification is soon tempered by the prospect of the first audit. Prior to an audit, many companies encounter significant difficulties, with the management team and quality department wading through a mountain of paper in order to prepare for the auditors.

---

1 See Appendix III for the full product suite.

Usually the FDA gives very little notice prior to an audit and has even been known to arrive unannounced. While a company may be producing a product to the correct standard, failure to demonstrate control over the documentation and change control process can give cause for failure of an FDA audit. This has in the past led to plant shut down, product withdrawal and the imposition of hefty fines.

Indeed the head of one large corporation was jailed following failure of an FDA inspection. Management fear of failure through non-conformance, coupled with the escalating cost of the document control process, was driving demand for focussed industry specific solutions.

THE GLOBAL IDM MARKET [2]

The total IDM market (including products and services) was forecast to be worth in excess of $10 billion by 2001, with a growth rate of 100% per annum between 1998 and 2001. Underpinning this growth was the installation in large organizations of integrated document management across the enterprise. In effect, since the first products were available over a decade ago and there had been many successful smaller projects, organizations could now see that document management had a real role to play in business efficiency. This was happening across many industries, pharmaceutical, banking, insurance and manufacturing, with products being installed in far more departments and business units than ever before.

This dramatic growth forecast, reflected an evolution of the industry since the first products became available in the late eighties. Over that period, a variety of technologies and products had been available in the area of basic document management. Many organizations installed products in departments, facilities and workgroups to solve particular problems. During this time changes had occurred in both the supply and demand side which had brought the sector to the fore for global I.T. managers.

---

2 Readers are recommended to refer to Appendix I: - The Global I.T. market, for a background on the dynamics within this industry.

DEMAND SIDE - THE BUYERS

Organization complexity and information sharing requirements had increased exponentially and this trend looked set to continue. It was estimated, that by the end of 1999, 75% of regularly used document based information would be held in digital form. This information was crucial to managing large dispersed organizations.

Managers had recently begun to view IDM as a potential means of managing these documents across the enterprise. At the same time ever increasing and cheaper levels of computer power were making it viable to install these products on standard platforms across the organization.

SUPPLY SIDE - THE SELLERS

The leading global I.T. companies had also seen this trend and some had begun to include basic document management functionality in their products (Microsoft with basic version control features in Word and in their E-mail products; IBM/Lotus with their product, Notes, which now includes specific document functionality).

In addition some of the competitors in the IDM area were maturing into significant companies with the capability to support large global users i.e. Documentum, File Net, Open Text.

QUMAS'S MARKET POSITION

| | Price / Functionality | |
	Low	High
Entire Market	Lotus Notes	Documentum File Net Open Text
Strategic Target		
Segment of Market		Nova Soft Qumas

IDM STANDARDS

Installing IDM enterprise-wide confronted pharmaceutical companies with complex issues. These related to defining their needs across the organization, choosing the right mix of products and technologies, selecting suppliers who would be around in five years time to support these solutions, and ensuring that they could be integrated into the existing infrastructure.

As outlined in the previous section and in Appendix I, market growth increased customer awareness in relation to the achievement of corporate standards. Enormous growth in the use of IDM highlighted to customers the need for inter-operability among the various document management products. Customers did not want to have a manufacturing plant in Cork using one system while an R & D facility in California used another. Without standards and standardization, organizations would be creating "islands" of information.

This goal, to have a homogenous corporate standard, was not entirely new. Some customers always had this objective. Indeed it was just such a demand that Documentum and the other enterprise-wide providers had been reacting to with their offerings. Documentum's sales strategy reflected this. Unlike Qumas, they tended to adopt a top-down approach, sales pitches were more likely to be made at client HQ to the directors of the I.T. department. Qumas on the other hand had been visiting quality assurance managers at the plant level. The strength of Qumas's approach was that they were meeting customers with very definite problems and they were offering them immediate solutions. For Qumas, this had compared favorably with the top-down strategy of convincing customers of the long-term strategic benefits of IDM. Qumas, as a result, was operating on a comparatively shorter sales cycle. Paul was convinced that the more definite benefits and shorter decision-making cycle had helped.

Recently, however, they were coming up against I.T. managers who were vetoing the Qumas option as it failed to comply with the increasing adoption of homogenous corporate standards. Customers were also pushing the industry to adopt a standard for communication between their systems.

THE "REGULATED" MARKET

The FDA-regulated industries (pharmaceutical, chemical, medical device, and biotech) were chosen as a target market as the sector was cash rich and traditionally invested in technology for business efficiency. The latter constituted a significant administrative, logistical and validation overhead. Qumas estimated that these organizations were spending approximately $4-5 billion annually on FDA compliance and related overhead. Digitized integrated document control presented a cost-effective solution to their document management problems. This is what Qumas did.

The potential for long term income from a customer was very significant with license extensions, implementation consultancy and an annual recurring license fee for use of the product. In addition a sale into an individual site opened the opportunity to roll the product out into the other sites in the client company. Typically the first sale into a client site was valued at $150,000, plus an annual software license fee (circa. 20% of the original sale value).

The U.S. was the most critical battlefield in the Qumas drive for market dominance. It constituted over 70% of the regulated industry with more than 90,000 FDA-regulated sites. Further market analysis identified more than 11,000 potential client sites for Qumas in the U.S. It was also a rapidly growing market. The primary factors driving market growth were: the move by regulatory bodies to cover wider areas and products, stricter environmental requirements leading to evermore regulatory legislation and pressure from the FDA to move towards electronic documentation. In addition, the increasing imperative of time to market in many of the regulated sectors was focussing attention on speeding the development and approval processes. IDM had obvious potential to contribute to this. This level of spend coupled with the fear and cost of failure ensured a significant incentive for users to look at strategies for reducing this cost and increasing the level of compliance. I.T. had a central role to play in this process and forecasted investment of $1 billion in software and services industry-wide over the next five years was not unreasonable.

Many U.S. pharmaceutical companies had relocated their manufacturing facilities outside the U.S. This move was an attempt to avail of attractive labour costs and tax regimes and to allow easy access to new markets prior to exporting back to the U.S. Indeed, it was just such considerations which had contributed to the emergence of the pharmaceutical production cluster in Ireland. The company's market research indicated that there were an additional 15,000 potential sites located outside the U.S.

In gaining major market share in the U.S. Qumas would automatically win market share at other geographical locations. This was because most global manufacturing facilities for the FDA-regulated sector, were part of U.S. corporations. Here also was where the FDA maintained stringent control with the most frequent policing of their compliance regulations. The U.S. environment was therefore more amenable to, and prepared to invest serious dollars in, a Qumas solution.

QUMAS'S COMPETITIVE ADVANTAGE

Qumas's application was specifically focused on the pharmaceutical industry's requirements - most of the other providers were marketing more generic products into a wide range of sectors. Ultimately, Qumas were looking to become leaders in the regulated market, satisfying 100% of the IDM needs of 100% of the customers in this segment.

In preparation for the Board meeting, Paul reflected on the factors which his experience and customer feedback suggested were the reasons for Qumas's success and strength. These conversations with customers appeared to boil down to some key points:

Focus
Qumas spoke the language of pharmaceutical quality and regulation, directly to the managers who understood and were responsible for the area. Unlike other players this was not just one of several markets, it was their sole focus.

Cost of Ownership
The Qumas team had built a product that matched and, in many cases, exceeded customer needs. They had developed a solution that could be installed quickly and cost

effectively - it did not involve large one to two year projects with expensive products and installation fees to consultants.

In some cases, competitors' customers were spending four times as much on consulting as they were on the products. With Qumas, however, it was regularly less than one third of the cost of the product. The larger, company wide solutions, being implemented by competitors, typically took much longer to specify, implement and operationalize. This meant that specific areas such as regulatory control might have to wait years for solutions that addressed their requirements.

Specific Features

In reviewing customer feedback and product income over the past three years, it was clear that there was one area of the Qumas portfolio that customers valued more than any other. The analysis showed that the document revision and control module accounted for 90% of sales. For buyers, this met their most pressing and complex needs. Tracking large documents across complex organizations with multiple contributors and users is a nightmare. Qumas was solving this real problem quickly. In product terms this appeared to be the primary source of competitive advantage.

Service

Clients simply liked the Qumas approach. They felt they were dealing with people working to solve their specific problems, not a large organization where queries and requests could 'disappear' anonymously. The words 'flexible' and 'responsive' were consistently used and had been key to winning increased business with existing customers.

SALES STRATEGY

Qumas's success had been built on their direct sales approach, combined with intimate industry knowledge. The problems the company were solving were well understood, to the extent that key senior executives were assigned responsibility for the area. Qumas targeted these executives directly and worked with them to influence the other key players in the organizations, e.g. I.T., Operations and Finance. Their direct marketing and branding were targeted at this group.

Although shorter than that of their competitors, the sales cycle tended to be long and protracted. This reflected the importance and value of the purchase to the client company. The timescale, from initial contact to receipt of order, could be anything from six to eighteen months. It necessitated a high level of interaction with the client, both at a technical and sales level. Many of the key staff within Qumas were actively engaged in the process. This usually involved various presentations at departmental and plant level, leading to a detailed proposal and final corporate presentation. After an order was sanctioned, lawyers from both sides had to agree contracts. Becoming a qualified supplier was a tough business.

As the Company won more sales, two things happened. Firstly, they became better at selling at this level. Secondly, as a consequence of their success and growth, they gained market credibility and legitimacy - there was far less focus now on the company, its relatively small size, and low resource base. Success bred success.

As a result of their approach, the sales and development team regularly met with potential clients, providing extensive and regular feedback for product development.

With their highly focused approach to the market, direct selling was again used in their entry to the U.S. and European markets.

U.S. MARKET ENTRY

The U.S. market was central to the company's long-term development plan. As part of the sales process to Irish sites and following direct targeting of specific U.S. companies, Qumas had been visiting the U.S. market regularly since 1995. However, it quickly became apparent that to establish real credibility in that market they needed a constant presence. Despite their low resource base, the company put one of their key Directors, Kevin O'Leary, into the U.S. full time in 1996. At the time, this was a difficult decision, given their limited human and financial resources. But it was seen as crucial to the future success of the company. By the end of his first year in the U.S., as a one-man operation, his efforts had accounted for much of the company's revenues and future sales prospect list.

Kevin's short-term objectives had been to build on Qumas's initial beachhead of accounts, with a view to rolling the product out to other sites within these companies and to use these accounts to leverage new business clients. This approach had been successful for Qumas in the past, with the result that one third of their new contracts were coming from existing clients implementing the products in new sites.

The sales process that Kevin engaged in was resource intensive. This limited the number of contacts he could handle. Also, his time was taken up in maintaining Qumas's profile through attendance at seminars and trade fairs. In addition, he had to manage the establishment of the U.S. office. Paul was acutely aware that Qumas needed a visible increase in their commitment to the US market, with additional dedicated sales, marketing and technical resources. Qumas had set a sales target for the U.S. of $50 million over the next five years. To achieve this they had budgeted to spend more than $2.5 million on their sales and marketing strategy in the U.S. over the next two years.

Kevin's energies were focused on developing contacts with Fortune 2000 rated companies in the relevant sectors. This market was, of course, also within the target market of their more broadly focussed and larger competitors[3].

Toward the end of 1998 two further seasoned executives from the company, David Cronin and Gerald O'Driscoll, relocated to the U.S. David set about establishing the West Coast Operation and Gerald joined Kevin on the East Coast. Paul also planned to recruit a further six additional sales staff, half of whom would be located in the West Coast sales office. The remainder of the budget was to be allocated to direct marketing, promotion in trade magazines and presentations at key trade fairs and seminars.

PARTNERSHIPS

Qumas needed to build a network of industry partners. This was a strategy that had been long pursued by competing companies, most obviously Documentum. Paul knew that the right

---

3 See Appendix 1

partnerships would be important to Qumas's future success. However, strategy in this area needed to be carefully balanced. While recognizing the potential for partnerships, Paul was keenly aware of the need to maintain direct relationships with customers - the key to the company's previous success. He was, therefore, reluctant to hand over the sales and marketing responsibility for any territory to a third party.

Paul was convinced of the merit of developing marketing partnerships with leading international I.T. consultancies such as Andersen and PwC and ERP[4] sellers such as Base 10; MFG Pro and BPICS who specialized in the pharmaceutical and related regulated market segments.

However, traditionally the large consultancies partnered with companies when they were obviously successful and on the way to a global market leading position. These companies also tended to generate a lot of consultancy income from product installation.

Paul felt that in time the market would reject the high cost approach and force the resellers to look at more cost-effective strategies, similar to those employed by Qumas.

In the interim, he was looking for partners among the new generation of highly specialized, focused and aggressive suppliers like Qumas and traditional players who did not see Qumas as a threat to their business. Paul knew, however, that the best marketing partners were looking at the same fundamental issue as the key buyers. Would this company be in a leading market position in five years time? Whatever strategy he pursued had to give partners and buyers this confidence.

THE COMPETITION

It was a widely held view, amongst providers of IDM solutions, that the market was about to experience a period of intense competition and consolidation. There was an expectancy that up to half the existing providers would either leave the industry, merge with larger providers, or be bought out. It was felt that this would happen despite continued growth in demand, as a small number of competitors emerged as the dominant

---

4 Enterprise Resource Planning is an integrated system of applications combining logistics, production, distribution order management, sales forecasting and financial and human resource management.

providers in the market. Paul had recently been reviewing the competition in anticipation of this market shakeout. The figure below outlines the primary attributes of some of the main competitors in the market.

OVERVIEW OF COMPETITORS

Company Name	Market Focus	Product Range	Product Type	Primary Sales Strategy
Qumas	Regulated Industries	Application Specific	Package	Direct Sales
Documentum	Universally Focused	Enterprise Wide	Tool-kit	Direct and Indirect Sales
NovaSoft	Pharmaceutical and Electronics Industries	Enterprise Wide	Tool-kit/ Package	Direct and Indirect Sales
Lotus	Universally Focused	Enterprise Wide	Tool-kit/ Package	Indirect Sales
FileNet	Universally Focused	Enterprise Wide	Tool-kit	Direct and Indirect Sales
OpenText	Universally Focused	Enterprise Wide	Tool-kit/ Package	Direct Sales
PC Docs	Universally Focused	Enterprise Wide	Package/ Tool-kit	Direct Sales
IXOS	Universally Focused	Enterprise Wide	Tool-Kit	Direct and Indirect Sales

DOCUMENTUM

Documentum was the leading global company for the supply of IDM solutions. It was a publicly-listed Corporation with a turnover in 1998 of over $100 million. The company consistently recorded impressive year on year growth through the1990s.

Documentum was marketed as a universally focused IDM product, targeted at a wide range of market sectors including Pharmaceutical, Electronics, and Financial Services. As with other universally focused companies, it was offering enterprise-wide solutions in these sectors. In the sector, Documentum was typically tackling larger problems across most of the functions in the organization including accounting, billing, marketing, production and R&D. Unlike Qumas it was not normally limited to the FDA-regulated aspects of the business.

Documentum had a leading presence in the marketplace, with a strong direct sales force. This approach was further supported by a strong list of partners who acted as system integrators, working closely with Documentum clients developing client applications. Documentum's partner list was impressive with over 40 service partners including key industry players such as Xerox and IBM. It had over 30 technology partners including SAP and its marketing partners included Microsoft, Hewlett-Packard, Sun Microsystems, Oracle and Netscape[5]. These partnership agreements ensured that Documentum was readily integrated with other solutions operating in the customer's organization. Consultancy houses were more than willing to recommend Documentum as it represented a significant opportunity for them to generate fees through implementation (these fees could often dwarf the "product" cost).

More recently, Documentum had acquired Relevance, a leading-edge provider of content mining technology for unstructured information. This "intelligent content mining" automatically analysed, categorised and delivered internal and external information to users in the context of their job function or areas of interest, thus accelerating business performance. This was part of Documentum's effort to position itself more broadly as a player in the Knowledge Management[6] market. This was seen as a means of differentiating Documentum by providing customers with products that managed the 'content' and 'know how' in the documents. In effect Documentum was expanding beyond the traditional IDM boundaries.

Documentum was the competitor that Qumas faced most frequently both in the US and Europe. Over the previous 5 years Documentum had become embedded in several of the leading Pharmaceutical Corporations where they had become the corporate standard. Despite this situation, Qumas had

---

5 A full list of Documentum's "Signature Partners" can be viewed at http://www.documentum.com/level_3.html?category=part&section=roster&item=roster.html

6 Knowledge Management is broader than Document Management and includes all efforts to increase company performance through improved utilisation of internal and external knowledge, experience and information.

been successful in tendering against Documentum amongst their client base in the pharmaceutical sector. Qumas saw their key competitive advantage as being the delivery to the customer of a package compared with Documentum's complex, resource-intensive software tool. The Qumas product took significantly shorter time to implement in the regulated industries (one to three months versus a year and more for Documentum). Qumas used this as a basis for differentiating themselves from their larger rivals such as Documentum. In effect, the selling proposition was based on Qumas's sectoral focus and lower implementation time and cost.

In competing against Documentum, Qumas's greatest difficulties related to its significantly smaller size and hence marketing power / market awareness. Also, in many cases, potential customers had already adopted Documentum. As Paul often noted "Qumas is always the right solution but not always the right product." In addition, Qumas had not been entirely successful in selling their solution as being corporate wide. To date, their successes had primarily been in manufacturing sites. This success had been a cause for optimism, given that in many instances these sites were in companies that had adopted Documentum at the corporate level[7]. In effect, Qumas had been chosen to solve the particular problems in the aspect of the business most prone to FDA regulation. However, the flip side of this was that Documentum was being adopted as the broader based solution or IDM Architecture. This worried Paul, as in the long term it could prove to be a serious threat to Qumas if Documentum chose to consolidate its position by squeezing out application specific and vertically focused competitors like Qumas.

On the up side, Paul knew that Documentum was primarily concentrated on the R&D facilities of these corporations and not strong on the manufacturing sites, where expenditure on IDM solutions had to be clearly justified on mission critical application requirements. In addition Documentum had moved on to other industry sectors which had weakened their focus on the FDA regulated industry sector.

---

7 60% of the Qumas client base had Documentum as their corporate standard for supply of IDM solutions.

NOVASOFT

Novasoft was marketing a universally focused, enterprise wide, tool kit solution through intermediaries. Paul had been happy with Qumas's ability to sell against NovaSoft. Paul felt that NovaSoft's relatively weak regulated industry knowledge had been key in Qumas's success against them. When pitching against Novasoft, Qumas highlighted the difficulty and costs associated with implementation of the Novasoft offering.

LOTUS NOTES

Lotus Notes, recently acquired by IBM, was a software solution that combined email, Internet, workflow and some document management features. It was built around basic organizational information sharing requirements i.e. telephone list, e-mail distribution, database sharing. It was from this background that Lotus attempted to move their product up the information value chain to a business type application. Paul felt that Lotus Notes was not as yet a true IDM system.

Lotus Notes targeted a very broad market and was not seen as presenting a real threat to Qumas if prospects were looking for a FDA-compliant solution. Paul felt that, where customers were not aware of Qumas, Lotus Notes had been chosen to attempt an internal solution. IBM was, however, aggressively selling (and in some cases giving virtually free) the product into their large customer base in an attempt to control that level of their customers' requirements.

THE FUTURE OPTIONS AND CHOICES

As he headed for home, Paul had plenty of reasons to be happy. With limited financial and human resources, Qumas's achievements in the US and European markets had been considerable. A solid foundation of clients, that now approached 50 sites across several continents, had adopted the product. Many clients were expanding their use of the product into new sites.

This client base was passionate about both Qumas "The Product" and Qumas "The Company". They included many of the leading corporations in the industry - Monsanto, Roche, Novartis, Schering Plough, Pharmacia & Upjohn and Bard. These clients provided Qumas with excellent references. Key partnerships had been formed in the industry with system integrators and software sellers. These included BaseTen, and Xerox. Qumas was regularly mentioned at industry events and seminars. Sales targets had been met over previous years, including on target earnings in their current fiscal year. Their client prospect list for the US exceeded $3.5 million. Competitors were now watching Qumas's every move.

Qumas had proven its ability to satisfy the needs of their target market. However it had, of late, become apparent to Paul and the other directors, that there were changes afoot in the market. These changes threatened the viability of the existing strategy.

As the market grew, customers were becoming increasingly concerned with the achievement of corporate standards. The incidence of IT managers vetoing Qumas's Document Revision Control product, was increasing of late. IT managers were insisting that the client site complied with whatever enterprise-wide solution was being adopted (as often as not, Documentum). Paul saw two possible alternative solutions to this dilemma.

The first option available was to build on the previous sales success that had been achieved with the Document Revision Control component of the Qumas product suite. This strategy would entail a concentration of the sales effort on Document Revision Control. In effect they would be attempting to increase market share by focusing on their strongest product. Pursuit of this strategy would necessitate the development of a much larger number of marketing partners to ensure industry wide representation beyond pharmaceuticals. The absence of such partners was now emerging as a limitation in the company's marketing effort. New customers could be sought from additional sites of existing clients and by getting new clients in pharmaceutical and other regulated sectors.

In pursuing this objective Qumas would be assisted by its latest product upgrade, Qumas Version 4. This latest version of the product differed from previous versions in that the Document Revision Control element was compatible with all of the competing products on the market. This was a crucial development in that it would allow Qumas to sell their Document Revision Control component easily into any company regardless of what IDM product operated as the corporate standard.

Because of Qumas's strategic focus on the regulated sector and their "package" strategy, their product could be readily added to Documentum or any of the other competing products. Qumas would be able to turn long time competitors into allies by providing a complementary, easily installed solution that could harness the power of any given IDM product to immediately handle the crucial area of document revision and control in the regulated sector.

The second option was to pursue share of customer rather than share of market. Faced with a situation where corporate-wide solutions were demanded, Qumas could seek to expand the amount of its product which each existing client took, and make the Qumas solution the client standard. While this would be a protracted process, the small number of companies that accounted for 70% of sites in the sector meant that it was achievable. This approach would also build on one of the company's key strengths – good relations with the current client base.

Paul favoured the first option on the grounds that it avoided having to take on their much larger competitors in head-to-head competition. Phil James, their European sales manager and a recent MBA graduate, felt they should pursue the second of these options. He was convinced of the need to "own" the customer. He was sure that Qumas could use their existing sites to prise open the small number of key accounts, allowing the company to sell in the remainder of the product suite. Conversations with customers had confirmed to Phil that the other products in the portfolio were as good as any on the market.

Like Kevin in the US, Phil had been successful in Europe in taking business from the larger competitors. Again, as in the US situation, existing Documentum customers in Europe had been won over by Phil's sales pitch with Qumas's Document Revision Control product. This, Phil argued, was strong evidence of the company's ability to compete directly for these customers. Added to this, the products that had been sold were proving highly successful and as a result good relations were being established with clients who trusted Qumas. On top of this, Phil was also worried about the prospect of being outflanked by the enterprise-wide providers, if Qumas were to adopt the first option and retain a narrow focus in the market.

Phil strongly believed they could become the IDM supplier

to their vertical market and several of the directors believed they should examine carefully the rationale behind this.

Paul also knew that whatever decision was made with regard to the company's future market position, there would be a need to finance this development. One option would be to try and go public, although Paul felt that the company was too small to do this in the short term. On the other hand, introducing new investors or venture capital into the company would reduce the percentage held by the promoters. This would, of course, be counterbalanced by the increased value of the company. Another alternative was to grow the company solely through sales revenue. The potential difficulty with this approach was that without initial scale, it would not have the credibility to win business rapidly enough to get a presence in the market. Without market presence, customer mind-share and organization experience developed through customer relationships, the pace of competition would leave the company behind.

There would be a vigorous debate around the issues at the board meeting. Paul was looking forward to it.

APPENDIX I

GLOBAL I.T. MARKET PLACE

I.T. is no different from any other industry although the product cycle times are faster and more aggressive. There are continual examples of companies that fail to recognize and embrace change in time to protect their franchise within their customer base, effectively destroying themselves to rebuild into a stronger market position.

A notable aspect of the market is that a relatively small number of customers have a fundamental influence. The world's top fifteen to twenty thousand organizations are the target of the leading global I.T. providers. Their buying decisions and behaviour dictate the future of some of the fastest growing companies (computer software and hardware) ever in the world of business.

Their decisions set the standards for the products and requirements for all corporate buyers. Acceptance by customers in this group is essential for a global I.T. company's success.

Over the past twenty years, I.T. has moved to the fore as a source of competitive advantage - the focus is moving from automating what you do, to enabling an organization to reduce costs and increasing differentiation. For example, I.T. has enabled the direct banking and insurance industry to exist, and new web technologies are now taking this to unprecedented levels of immediacy, accessibility and cost.

A further illustration of the importance of I.T. is its role in relation to mergers and acquisitions - in many cases if the respective organizations cannot quickly integrate at the I.T. level, many of the potential synergies are never realized.

Billion dollar businesses in products and services have developed around meeting these needs. From Microsoft, SAP and Oracle in software to Hewlett Packard, Compaq and Sun in hardware and Andersen Consulting, EDS, and Logica in services and consulting, the stakes are high.

I.T. and business managers of these organizations are the focus of some of the most aggressive sales and marketing campaigns ever for new waves of products, services and technologies from both new and established providers. Contracts are for the long term and can run into tens of millions of dollars.

For buyers the issues are complex. There is pressure to develop the "perfect solution" meeting precisely the organization's needs - in effect, taking software development tools and developing everything internally. This may be satisfactory for smaller projects but on a larger scale the risk is significant, moving management focus from the business and creating enormous I.T. departments, effectively moving the organization into the I.T. business!

IT managers face the dilemma of keeping 100% of the internal users happy 100% of the time with a limited budget against a background of changing business and technology environments. As a result, buyers look for mechanisms to "share" this pressure by setting corporate standards and looking for best of breed specialists in product and service providers. This approach enables them to maximize the use of their resources by moving the role of I.T. in the organization to that of strategist, architect and project manager. This approach enables these buyers to take advantage of the specialist companies' continued investment in R&D and experience gained from other customers. In return, they accept less than optimum functional solutions that are, however, supported by established and successful sellers and referenced by use in other similar organizations.

This process of standardization takes place at various levels and is supplemented by in-house development on smaller projects.

Hardware	These range from Mainframes, Mini-computers and
Operating Systems	PCs from vendors like IBM, HP, Compaq, Sun,
Development Tools	Dell etc. Operating Systems are available from these companies in addition to Microsoft.
Networking and Communications	Local area network technology connecting plants and offices sourced from Microsoft, Novell etc. In international communication, technologies are available from Cisco, Lucent, Nortel etc.

Office / Personal Productivity Products	Products installed on every P.C. similar to Word and Excel from Microsoft, Lotus, Korell etc.
Information Sharing Platforms	E-mail and related products again installed in every P.C. in the organization. Major companies in this area are Microsoft, Lotus, Netscape, Novell etc.
Database	Standards for holding key corporate and customer information from companies such as Oracle, IBM, Infomix, Sybase, and Microsoft.
Business Transaction Applications	Enterprise resource planning applications (ERP) catering for the major business functions such as purchasing, manufacturing, distribution, finance and H.R. Key providers here are SAP, Peoplesoft, Baan, Oracle etc.
Consulting, Service Facilities Management Companies	Consulting and development services to assist organisations understanding their business and I.T. requirements, choose the appropriate products and develop a company-wide solution. Key players are Andersen Consulting, EDS, KPMG, PWC, etc.

Within the above structure there is also a requirement for a wide range of industry and problem specific products and solutions. This supports a range of very significant, but more niche providers e.g. Misys in banking and financial sectors.

Within each area, there is intense competition as providers compete to own that level of the market. Increasingly, as the providers seek higher growth rates, they add and integrate more functionality into their products. As a result, they can encroach into other levels in attempts to dominate the total market, e.g. Microsoft and Oracle.

Equally, the market is replete with both loose and close

alliances between key players at each level e.g. SAP and Andersen Consulting, SAP and Oracle, Microsoft and Compaq etc.

There is also a constant stream of new products and technologies from start-up companies competing to enter this tough, but potentially lucrative, market. They are looking for opportunities to prove themselves with smaller more open organizations and pilot projects. Many fail outright, some ideas are absorbed into the product strategies of the mainstream providers, and in a few cases new global potential players evolve. Ten years ago Oracle, SAP and Compaq were minor players and leaders at that time such as DEC and Unyses have all but disappeared, while others such as IBM have been forced to continually re-invent themselves to stay ahead. More recently this process has been apparent with a new generation of companies emerging in the area of sales and marketing automation and Internet technologies. Siebel, Vantive, Carify and Broad Vision and Netscape are all companies that did not exist five years ago.

THE ROLE OF INTEGRATED DOCUMENT MANAGEMENT

Over the past decade a variety of technologies and products have been available in the area of basic document management. Many organizations installed early products in departments, facilities and workgroups to solve particular problems. Through this period changes have occurred in both the supply and demand side and have brought the sector to the fore for global I.T. managers.

DEMAND SIDE - THE BUYERS

Organization complexity and information-sharing requirements have increased exponentially and this trend is set to accelerate. By year end 1999 it is estimated that 75% of regularly used document-based information will be held in digital form. This information in these documents is crucial to managing large dispersed organizations.

Managers have recently begun to view IDM as a potential means of managing this information across the enterprise. At the same time ever increasing and cheaper levels of computer power make it viable to install these products on standard platforms across the organization.

SUPPLY SIDE - THE SELLERS

The leading global I.T. providers have also seen this. Some have begun to include basic document management functionality in their products (Microsoft with basic version control features in Word and their E-mail GroupWare products, Lotus with their product, Notes, which now includes specific document functionality.

In addition some of the companies in the IDM area have matured into significant companies with the capability to support large global users i.e. Documentum, File Net, Open Text.

CONCLUSION

IDM technology has matured, dominant providers have emerged and customers realize the business benefits available to companies that install IDM across the enterprise.

The pharmaceutical and regulated sectors are similar to other global industries with respect to the adoption of IDM. They have also used products in individual projects and facilities, perhaps more so than any other sector.

Installing IDM enterprise-wide confronts them with complex issues in relation to defining their needs across the organization, choosing the right mix of products and technologies, selecting providers who will be around in five years time to support these solutions and ensuring they can be integrated into the existing infrastructure.

Within the pharmaceutical sector forces relating to:

• Increasing levels and reducing costs of product innovation
• Reducing cost and time to market
• Globalization and consolidation

set the agenda of strategic decision making across the business.

APPENDIX II

SAMPLE CLIENT LIST

Customer	Location	Parent
Yansen	Ireland	Johnson and Johnson
FMC	Ireland, Brussels, Delaware	FMC Corp.
Roche	Ireland and New Jersey	Roche
Howmedica	Ireland	Phizer Group
Schering Plough	Ireland	Schering Plough Corp
Becton Dickinson	Ireland	Becton Dickinson
Bard Medical		CR Bard Corp
Protiva	Belgium	Monsanto
Monsanto	Saint Louis, U.S.A.	Monsanto
Cambridge Life Sciences	U.K.	BMW Germany
Pharmacia and Upjohn	Ireland	Pharmacia and Upjohn
Novartus	Austria	Novartus
Fedara*	Belgium	Fedara
Nova Nordisk*	Denmark	Nova Nordisk
Pharmacia Upjohn*	Puerto Rico and Italy	
Bard	Boston, Salt Lake City, Mexico, Texas	CR Bard

(* Denotes sale through partner)

APPENDIX III

THE QUMAS PRODUCT SUITE

Product	Function
Document Revision Control	Automates management of the document revision process
Corrective Actions and Non-conformance	Automates incident logging, investigations, corrective actions and quality sign-off
Vendor Analysis	Monitors, tracks and analyses suppliers to ensure that they conform to pre-set criteria.
Customer Query and Complaint Management	Captures all complaint details on line, automatically routes complex issues to correct department and keep your clients informed by means of automated fax updates. Identifies recurring problems, regular complaints and other trends.
Control Module	The hub around which each of the application modules operates, either individually or collectively

These Products had been upgraded three times since 1995 as a result of continuing investment in R & D. This R & D accounted for 50% of the company's total annual overhead.

APPENDIX IV

SUMMARY FINANCIAL INFORMATION

Historic Sales/Profit

To protect commercially sensitive information actual figures
are not used. However, the relationships between the individual items are reflective of those typically seen in high growth
software companies, in the business-to-business sector, at this
stage of their development.

SALES /PROFIT
('000's Dollars)

	1996	1997	1998
Sales	$640	$1200	$2400
Profit	($200)	($380)	($900)

Forecasts for the next 3 years
('000's Dollars)*

	1999	2000	2001
Sales	6500	14000	25000
Cost of Sales	1170	2100	2500
R&D	3800	7300	8000
Sales & Marketing	2100	3200	5000
Management & Admin	1200	1600	2100
Capital Expenditure	200	700	1500
Profit	(770)	(900)	5900

*These projections had been developed by the management at
their last review, six months prior to the board meeting.

*The financial information in this section is provided as a
yearly forecast, to enable managers to focus on the key
business drivers and the revenues and expenses associated with them.*

Blooming Clothing : The Case for Renewal

Edel Foley[1]

INTRODUCTION

"When the going gets tough, the tough get going." Martha O'Byrne hummed along with the song on the car radio. Battling with the Dublin city traffic, she reflected on how the song mirrored her own business situation. As managing director of Blooming Clothing, a small Irish clothing firm, she had led the business since its inception in 1995. Now it was spring 1999, and the millennium was just a matter of months away. The vibrant Dublin streetscape certainly showed off the current economic prosperity. It was a good time to think about renewal, new opportunities, and expansion to new markets. These would be the themes for the strategy meeting scheduled for this afternoon. "Let the good times roll," she murmured, as the traffic lights changed to green.

BLOOMING CLOTHING: A SHORT HISTORY

Blooming Clothing was established in 1985 by O'Byrne and two other partners. The aim was to specialise in a niche of the women's outerwear market: maternity wear. The company started business with a retail outlet in Dublin and sold maternity wear under the Blooming label, which it outsourced through local suppliers. When this arrangement proved unsatisfactory, Blooming turned to manufacturing its own lines. By spring of 1999, the firm employed fifty people at a factory in the Liberties, an historic part of central Dublin, and a move to a newly built premises nearby was imminent. Ten other employees were attached to the retail operations of the company.

At this point in time, the firm had established a dominant position in Ireland, selling through its own retail outlet, a range

---

1 The author wishes to acknowledge the kind assistance of Martha O'Byrne, Blooming Clothing, in the preparation of this case study.

of independent boutiques, and a concession arrangement with five of the Mothercare outlets in the Republic. In the UK the Blooming label was to be found in Harrods of London, and in the John Lewis stores. Sample turnover and financial data for the company can be seen in Appendix 1.

The firm felt that it had now established itself as a high quality supplier of branded maternity wear in the Irish and UK markets. Having survived the turbulence and recessionary phases of the markets that characterised the early 1990s, management now considered that it was in a good position to capitalise on the strong surge in the economic environment. And, contrary to the original forecasts, the birth rate in most of Western Europe was holding up well. With turnover at the £2m mark, it was now time to shape a strategy that would ensure prosperity in the years ahead.

THE MANAGEMENT TEAM

Day to day management responsibilities were divided between three people. Martha O'Byrne was managing director and also took responsibility for sales and marketing. June Boore was in charge of design and production management. Liz O'Byrne was responsible for finance and retail operations.

With the experience accumulated in running the company through good times and bad, this core team felt it had a good base of skills. However, the day to day management of operations gave rise to several difficulties. The issues involved in keeping the factory going - sourcing supplies, filling orders and dealing with customers - took up a lot of everyone's time. The necessity to travel and be away from one's desk for a couple of days at a stretch meant that, on return, there was a list of problems pressing for management attention. In common with other firms in the clothing industry, management perceived a need for more formal, off the job training, but found it difficult to spare the time away from the day to day responsibilities of running the business.

The management team was in strong agreement about the company's own unique knowledge about the industry, the technology, and about its own particular niche of the market. At recent board meetings, the team had discussed how larger clothing companies such as Benetton had used their core knowledge as the key to expansion and integration of the organisation. The management of Blooming wondered how its own unique knowledge could be used to plot the future direction of the company.

THE PRODUCT

Blooming Clothing offered maternity wear in a range of formal and casual styles. The objective was to offer a selection of lines that would suit all occasions, so that a customer could find all her needs satisfied by the one label. Collections were launched twice a year, in Spring and Autumn. (See sample brochure: Appendix 2).

Blooming's designs were regarded as being at the high price, high fashion end of the market. The label was geared towards the more affluent and fashion-conscious woman, who was, most likely, in the workplace, and needed a range of outfits to see her through her pregnancy. The company noticed that sales of the Autumn collection were better than those for the Spring, and speculated that Spring and Summer wear, being more casual, could be bought from a wide range of outlets, not necessarily those specialising in maternity wear.

THE CONSUMER

In marketing terms, maternity wear fits the description of an unsought good:

> "Goods that the consumer does not know about or knows about but does not normally think of buying.....The classic examples of known but unsought goods are life insurance, cemetery plots, gravestones and encyclopaedias."
>
> *(Kotler, 1994:436)*

In other words, here was a product aimed at the women's market and at a situation-specific niche, that is, all expectant mothers. The life of the product was relatively short: once a pregnancy was over maternity wear was no longer necessary.

From observation, it was evident that pregnant women relied on a range of sources for clothes. One possibility was to buy a size or two larger from any conventional retailer. Outfits could be borrowed from friends and family members. However,

from its own research, Blooming knew that specialist maternity wear was more sought after by the second time mother, who
appreciated the specialised tailoring and comfort of fit. The
challenge was how to communicate this benefit to the younger
first-time mother; whose perception of maternity wear was of
dull, frumpy outfits seriously lacking in any element of fashion.

Attitudes towards pregnancy had seen enormous change.
The older picture was of a woman in the home, who disguised
her pregnancy as much as possible. Now, most women in the
childbearing age group all over Europe were in the work force.
Pregnancy was an event to be celebrated and flaunted; recently several well-known media figures had featured in women's
magazines, celebrating their expectant state. Marital status
was no longer an issue; in most European states an average of
one in five births were to single parents. The immediacy of the
Millennium was also forecast to have a positive influence on
the birth rate.

TABLE 1: RELEVANT SOCIAL TRENDS IN EUROPE, 1996

	Fertility rate	**Economically Active Women**	**Birth rate**
	children born, per female	*% of female population*	*per 000 inhabitants*
Austria	1.4	42.8	10.9
Belgium	1.6	42.3	11.4
Denmark	1.6	45.3	12.9
France	1.7	45.2	12.6
Ireland	1.9	37.7	13.6
Italy	1.2	36.9	9.3
Netherlands	1.5	41.5	11.8
Spain	1.2	38.3	11.0
United Kingdom	1.8	43.8	12.6

(Euromonitor, 1998)

THE MARKET

While the 1980s and early 1990s had seen the age of first time mothers move upwards, the trend of the late 1990s was that mothers were getting younger. This trend was thought to be influenced by three elements: strong economic circumstances throughout Europe, a loosening of social mores, and medical information suggesting that younger mothers presented a significantly lower level of health risk.

These younger mothers-to-be were very fashion conscious, but less willing to pay a premium price for clothing than their more mature counterparts. Being at the "nest - building" stage, they were often taking on additional financial commitments in anticipation of family needs. They wanted clothes that were up to the minute, of good quality, at a competitive price. They were as likely to select a larger size from their usual brands of clothing as to seek out specialist maternity wear lines. They shopped along the high street, and were unwilling to detour or make special trips elsewhere. As they were busy at work, they were under some time pressure and willing to use catalogues and other ordering systems.

TABLE 2: THE WOMEN'S OUTERWEAR MARKET, EUROPE, 1996

	US Dollars, per capita
Austria	433.0
Belgium	377.6
Czech Republic	105.2
Denmark	350.9
France	180.0
Germany	341.4
Ireland	192.5
Italy	162.0
Slovakia	181.3
Spain	148.1
United Kingdom	248.1

(Euromonitor, 1998)

THE "BLOOMING" BRAND

Since the establishment of the company in 1985, Martha O'Byrne and her management team had been very conscious of the need for a strong brand impact if the firm was to succeed in the market. As a business graduate and then an investment banker, she had witnessed the failure of businesses that did not take the branding message to heart.

The initial awareness of the name "Blooming" was through its own retail outlet in South Leinster Street, Dublin. Located on the fringes of Dublin's premier shopping district, and beside the University of Dublin, the signage and design of the shop gave a clear indication of what was within. (See Appendix 3). As the firm started to manufacture its own lines, the Blooming logo was used on the labels and swing tickets on the garments. Special bags and tissue wrapping were supplied to retailers and concessionaires. A new brochure was produced for every seasonal collection.

The brand's qualities were perceived to be quality, individuality, uniqueness of design and the fact that it was made in Ireland. Blooming had turned down offers to produce private label lines for other retailers and manufacturers. It was proud of the fact that it was the only branded clothing stocked by Mothercare in Ireland: all other clothing stocked by Mothercare children's and women's range was under its own labels.

So far, the Blooming brand had received a positive response in the Irish and UK markets. O'Byrne and her partners felt that the brand would be of even greater importance if the broader European market were to be addressed. Branded clothing was of more importance to mainland European retailers than was the case in the UK, and European retailers sought to stock distinct ranges of easily recognised brands and labels which made their customers' shopping decisions easier.

THE COMPETITION

In the generic sense, Blooming's competitors spanned a wide field: manufacturers of conventional ladies outerwear, manufacturers of larger sizes and suppliers of specialist maternity wear. The nature and style of competition had moved along dramatically during the 1990s. (See Appendix 4: The Irish

Clothing Industry: Shaping up for Change). Some retailers were now sourcing their own private labels of maternity wear at competitive prices. More significant though, was the arrival of European brands to the UK and Irish markets. These brands, operating on a large scale of business, were able to offer good prices and strong marketing support. The department stores and boutiques, which, ten years ago, would have only stocked the Blooming brand as their range of maternity wear, were now stocking two or three European labels alongside it. These new competitors had appointed regional agents in the markets and were offering good levels of service and support with their brands.

Blooming viewed the competition to be emanating from three sources: branded maternity wear being sold through the independent boutiques and department stores, own branded merchandise being sold through chains and department stores, and new specialist European chains which were establishing in Ireland and the UK. At present, the company felt that there were five such competitors across the range with a significant presence in its markets.

ROCHES STORES

This Irish owned group of department stores was currently reviving its fortunes after going through a period of low profits and consolidation of activities. Its clothing section carried a mixture of manufacturers' brands on a concession basis and private labels. In Spring 1999, it launched its own range of maternity wear under the label "Expectations." The designs were fashionable and the prices moderate.

BENETTON

This Italian, family-owned clothing group had extended throughout Europe using the franchise route. It carried lines of bright, colourful, casual clothing aimed at the young and young at heart. It was famous for its advertising campaigns, which had generated worldwide controversy and publicity. It carried a limited range of maternity wear in its higher traffic outlets. Prices were regarded as mid-market, designs and fabrics were simple, in line with the rest of the Benetton range.

DOROTHY PERKINS

This UK-owned chain operated throughout Britain and Ireland, through a combination of its own stores and concession outlets in department stores. The chain offered a wide range of maternity wear styles under its own label. Quality was regarded as poor and prices were low. Dorothy Perkins' advertising was conducted on an umbrella basis for the whole group. High quality brochures were used to promote different collections.

FORMES

This French-designed label sold through independent outlets and through its own group of stores in France, Belgium and the UK. In 1998 it opened its first Irish outlet, in Dublin. Design was sharp and covered a range of smart and casual maternity styles. Pricing was at the middle to upper range of the market, and quality was considered to be high.

MOTHERCARE

This specialist chain operated over 300 stores in the UK, Europe, and the Middle and Far East. This included eight stores in the Republic of Ireland. Research in the UK had shown that at least nine out of ten mothers-to-be visit Mothercare at some stage during their pregnancy.

This chain stocked two separate ranges of maternity wear in its Irish stores. The Blooming range was carried on a concession basis with its own clearly designated space and display racks. The Blooming company was particularly proud of the fact that theirs was the only manufacturer branded clothing stocked by Mothercare.

The second range was Mothercare's own maternity range, which sold under the brand name "Tomorrow." The range focused on casual everyday wear, and design was regarded as dull. Prices and quality were middle of the range.

Mothercare relied on its own catalogue and on word of mouth for most of its promotional activity. The store format was currently regarded as somewhat tired and in need of a fresh approach.

MARKETING AND PROMOTION

As a typical small company, Blooming did not have any one person responsible for marketing. Management resources were focused on production. If buyers did not receive their orders on time, sales would suffer.

The managing director herself undertook most of the marketing work, in consultation with the other directors. O' Byrne also took on responsibility for sales, which entailed establishing contact and making presentations to key store buyers. The company produced a brochure twice a year, alongside its new collections. This was distributed through all sales outlets, and to doctors' waiting rooms and maternity hospitals.

The firm's own shop in South Leinster Street acted as a flagship for the brand. It had a heavily branded shopfront and window display. Inside, the store layout and design reflected an upmarket image: so much so that some callers were surprised to find that the garments that attracted them inside were maternity wear only.

At the point of sale in all retail outlets, Blooming used branded card displays and brochures to highlight the merchandise. Purchases were wrapped in branded tissue paper and placed in a carrier bag bearing the firm's logo.

Blooming did little advertising in its own right. It gave boutiques a credit towards any advertising or promotion undertaken for the brand. O'Byrne herself commented, "In marketing terms, I would give us one and a half out of ten at the moment. But we have succeeded with what we have done so far."

SUPPLY CHAIN MANAGEMENT

The clothing industry, in common with the food industry, relied on a complex chain of interdependencies to pull its goods through from the point of manufacture to the point of sale to the final customer.

FIGURE 1: SUPPLY CHAIN RELATIONSHIPS IN THE CLOTHING INDUSTRY

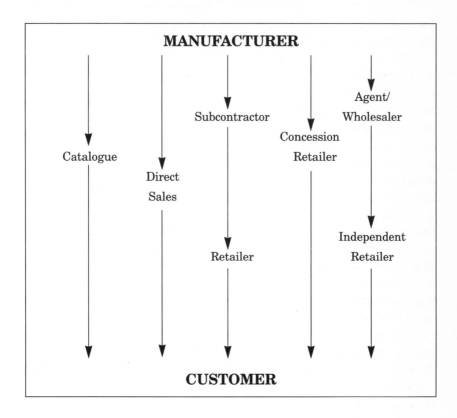

The relationships shown in Figure 1 demonstrate the range and depth of supply chain relationships in the clothing industry. At the simplest level, the manufacturer could produce directly for a customer or group of customers. This happens at both ends of the market: bespoke design and contract manufacture. The next alternative is to use an agent or wholesaler as an intermediary. In the UK, the agent was the typical arrangement used by exporters to that market, and each agent was responsible for a particular territory or customer group. In Europe, the scale of business was larger. Clothing agents and wholesalers were grouped together in a particular business centre, which typically had showrooms and exhibition space. This facilitated buyers, who could see a wide range of potential suppliers in one area. For the vendors, there were obvious syn-ergies from being clustered together, in terms of costs, infor-mation sharing, peer learning, fashion shows and PR. In some cases there were tax advantages, which further reinforced the barriers to potential entrants outside the system.

Clothing retailers were broadly of two types: the chain stores and the independent boutiques. Chain stores had strong buying muscle and were usually keen to get good value and keep or improve their own margins. They sought good design without compromising too much on quality. Mindful of the high street casualties from recessions of the eighties, the modern chain retailer was ruthless in evaluating the contribution of every label in the store. Operating the DPP (Direct Product Profitability) system, lines which did not perform were quickly dropped from a chain's range, leaving an opportunity for new entrants. The experience of Blooming in its relationship with chain stores was positive. It found that once it secured the con-fidence of the store buyer, it was able to process orders effi-ciently and payment terms were good. The key was to pick the chains that were looking for new labels and were strong and well managed enough to survive threats to their business.

The situation with the independent retailers was different again. Boutiques were typically one - shop operations man-aged by the owner. These outlets were usually serviced by manufacturers' agents. Boutique owners valued personal con-tact, and often felt that this element was lacking in their rela-tionship with agents, who were focused on generating sales to make their own commission. The manufacturer did not have direct contact with the independent boutiques, other than to service the orders passed on through agents. This sector was expanding in numbers, as provincial towns were experiencing the demand for as fashionable a range of clothing as was to be found in the cities. Blooming had built a good sales network through general and specialist boutiques, but was now finding that other European suppliers of maternity wear were approaching these retailers. Boutiques which ten years ago would have exclusively carried the Blooming range were now stocking two or three other brands, in response to availability and a perceived demand for more choice and a wider range of price points. From a financial viewpoint, supplying the boutiques with merchandise incurred high overheads on delivery costs and agency commissions.

INTERNATIONAL MARKETS

From start-up, management at Blooming was aware of the need to seek new markets, and the relative size of the Irish market was also a strong impetus to move abroad. Like most other Irish companies, Blooming initially looked at the UK market. Over time, it had built up contacts and sales in chain stores owned by John Lewis, Mothercare, Harrods and Miss Selfridge. The business in this market was handled through a London based agent, Gwenda Favoro, with which the company had a long standing and satisfactory relationship. For the future, it was targeting John Lewis as the chain with the strongest prospects for business development. The firm was also actively seeking agents in Scotland and Northern Ireland to develop business in those regions. The UK's nonparticipation in the Euro currency was causing problems in price negotiations and profit forecasts for that market.

Blooming had travelled further in search of business. Agents had been appointed in Sweden and Belgium in 1994, but these markets were in recession then and sales were disappointing. In 1995, orders were filled from a Japanese agent, but there were major differences in sizing which took some time to sort out. The slide in the value of the yen made the market unattractive, and Blooming did not pursue any further business there.

In January 1999, the company took a stand at a specialist European clothing trade fair in Cologne. It had two objectives in mind: to generate orders and to eyeball the competition. En route to the trade fair, disaster struck, with half of the collection being stolen. Undeterred, the company exhibited at the show and came away with a strong positive feeling that its designs could match any of the Europeans for style and for price. It vowed to return to Cologne next year, and looked forward to a stronger impact with a complete collection.

MANUFACTURING AND OUTSOURCING

At present, Blooming manufactures its designs from its own factory, with a workforce of fifty people. The company relies on the CMT (cut, make and trim) system, whereby designs are made and finished in-house. In 1995, it hired two new young designers who made strong improvements to this aspect of the range.

In common with the rest of the Irish clothing industry, the company was keenly aware of the global trend towards outsourcing of manufacturing, particularly to lower cost countries in Eastern Europe, Asia and North Africa. For a small company, this presented logistical difficulties, but the bigger players in the clothing industry were marching ahead and in some cases were already outsourcing their entire manufacturing requirement. This would leave an organisation free to concentrate on design, branding and product development. For a smaller company, there was also the possibility of outsourcing closer to home, using one or several CMT houses. Blooming was already outsourcing knitwear from an Italian company.

Another perceived change in the market was in the relationship between clothing retailers and their suppliers. The relationship was moving from one of distance to closer interdependency. Retailers were reducing the number of suppliers on their contract lists, and looking for mutual trust in return for mutual benefits and partnerships. There was also a perceptible move towards more own-labels, leaving the individual supplier with less room to manoeuvre. Small clothing companies stood to benefit from this change if they had the internal strengths and knowledge base to offer the foundations to a partnership.

THE CASE FOR RENEWAL

Management at Blooming was pleased with the progress the company had made to date. To have survived thus far in such a competitive industry was in itself an achievement.

But the directors appreciated that there was little room for complacency. "In a sense," O'Byrne reflected, "the boat has already gone out. The weaker players in this market have been eliminated." The home market was more competitive and growing in strength. The European market was going through a phase of consolidation, but Blooming felt that it could match any of the players it had seen in the competition there. The move to a new premises offered the opportunity to grow sales, and bring in new ideas. To be a stronger player in the market, the firm would need to push for higher turnover. A two-pronged marketing strategy was needed, to defend existing markets and to develop new ones. It was time to start making decisions, and to plot a new growth strategy.

APPENDIX 1:
COMPANY TURNOVER AND FINANCIAL DATA

YEAR	TURNOVER, IR£M
1994	**1.4**
1995	**1.5**
1996	**1.7**
1997	**1.85**
1998	**1.9**

BALANCE SHEET AS AT 31 OCTOBER, 1997, IR£

FIXED ASSETS	
Tangible assets	101,448
Financial Assets	30,000
	131,448
CURRENT ASSETS	
Stocks	278,823
Debtors and prepayments	252,892
Cash at bank and in hand	105,919
	637,634
CREDITORS (due within 1 year)	(429,868)
NET CURRENT ASSETS	207,776
TOTAL ASSETS LESS CURRENT LIABILITIES	339,214
CREDITORS (Due after more than 1 year)	(12,954)
GOVERNMENT GRANTS	(14,306)
TOTAL NET ASSETS	311,954
Financed by:	
CAPITAL AND RESERVES	
Called up share capital	287,143
Profit and loss account	(25,189)
TOTAL SHAREHOLDERS FUNDS	261,954
SUBORDINATED LOAN	50,000
TOTAL CAPITAL EMPLOYED	311,954

APPENDIX 2: SAMPLE BROCHURE

APPENDIX 3: THE "BLOOMING" SHOPFRONT

APPENDIX 4: THE IRISH CLOTHING INDUSTRY: SHAPING UP FOR CHANGE.

"The Irish Clothing sector is in the process of transition from being a traditional manufacturing industry to being an industry that is relatively knowledge-intensive, and makes use of a variety of professional skills."
(McIver Consulting, 1998)

During 1990-1998 the Irish clothing industry experienced a period of consolidation and change. This appendix describes the influences on change, the key drivers for competitiveness, and current and proposed strategic priorities.

INDUSTRY PROFILE

Employment in the clothing industry decreased by 15% between 1990 and 1996. By 1996 the industry was employing 13,200 people, representing about 6.7% of total manufacturing employment. The loss in employment was caused by company closures, most of which occurred during 1990-1993, due to the crisis in exchange rates between Ireland and the UK. The clothing trade, being very reliant on the UK market, and operating on low margins, was one of the main casualties of the crisis.

The Irish clothing industry has a relatively small share of its home market - an estimated share of 15% in 1996 - but is a strong exporter. In 1996, 86% of clothing output was exported.

Dependence on the UK market has loosened since 1993, and it now accounts for 63% of clothing exports. Other significant markets are Germany, France, Switzerland and Spain.

Pay in the industry is lower than in other manufacturing sectors, reflecting the reality that the value added per employee is lower than in other more modern and less labour-intensive manufacturing sectors. However, there are indications that companies in the sector are becoming stronger, albeit at a slower rate than the average for Irish industry as a whole. In 1996, Forbairt, the state support agency responsible for indigenous industry, launched an initiative for the clothing sector called *Securing the Future*. It proposes improving competitiveness by focusing on three strands:

• A Competitiveness Improvement Programme (CIP).

- The Irish Garment Technology Centre - seminars and projects, supported by EU and State funding.
- Support for Design and R&D programmes.

During 1992 -1996, Forbairt paid grants totalling IR£13.8 m. to clothing firms. Areas of support included improvements in manufacturing systems, computer aided design (CAD), and recruitment of designers.

Support for international sales was channelled through Enterprise Ireland. Specific supports included the Market Development Fund, Targeted Marketing Consultancy and Marketing Activity Investment Support. During 1992 - 1997, the Irish Trade Board, the precursor of Enterprise Ireland, invested IR£9.8 m. in the clothing sector.

Training support was provided by FAS - the Industrial Training Authority. Specific training programmes were put in place to cover machinists, production management, design and marketing. These initiatives cost almost IR£3 m. during the period 1991 - 1995. The industry was very positive about training, but many programmes ran with fewer participants than intended. FAS had to postpone or cancel some events due to companies being unable to manage without key staff.

Agency interventions were regarded as playing an important role in bringing about change in the industry. Key areas were the prominence now given to design, and increased use of CAD techniques.

FACTORS INFLUENCING CHANGE
While it would be simplistic to isolate direct cause-and-effect relationships, several factors were important to the clothing industry environment during the 1990s.

Changing Economic Conditions
As Ireland became a more developed economy, labour costs rose, particularly affecting labour intensive industries such as clothing. Lower cost economies in Eastern Europe, Morocco, China and India were now the new players for labour intensive industries. In Eastern Europe and Morocco, the clothing industry was upgrading itself to become an equal player with firms in Western Europe.

Labour Market Shortages

Traditionally, the clothing industry recruited young women on low rates of pay, particularly when compared with more modern manufacturing. With a more buoyant employment situation, clothing companies were now experiencing more difficulty in recruiting and retaining staff. For management, this raised problems with productivity and with upgrading to higher technologies which depended on more skilled people.

Outsourcing

The practice of outsourcing production, mainly to Eastern Europe and North Africa, had become prevalent in the European clothing industry since 1991. Irish companies, for reasons of their own, had been slow to follow this trend. The savings on production costs were reduced by transport costs and by management time needed to co-ordinate between locations. Lead times were long and more suited to large-scale production. However, with the labour shortage becoming acute, Irish companies were re-evaluating the situation. For the future, many were considering using their own production base for short runs, urgent orders and samples, and outsourcing the larger, longer term business.

Design & Branding

Since 1991, many companies have improved their branding and marketing resources. The number of professional designers working in the industry has doubled. Companies have worked to establish and strengthen brands, with a few key firms integrating forward into retailing.

Retail Chains in Ireland

Chain stores from the UK and mainland Europe had made significant inroads in the Irish market. These chains usually locate their purchasing function in their home country offices. They rely on global sourcing and large volumes to keep prices keen. For Irish suppliers, access to these buying centres, price, and production capacity are problem areas. The result is that a growing sector of the Irish clothing market is almost closed off to Irish suppliers. The other effect of the chain stores is to put pressure on the independent retailers, which have been good customers for Irish fashion. The prospect of an economic slow-down would make the independents vulnerable.

Technological Change

The industry had widely adapted to CAD techniques, but CAM (Computer Aided Manufacturing) was less common, as it required a reasonable level of scale to be cost-effective. The more technologically adept clothing firms were considering integrating information from production, logistics and finance systems. This was considered a key issue in the context of supply chain management, which calls for better communication and information for supply partnerships.

THE FUTURE

The industry view is currently positive, and it is felt that most clothing firms have improved in technology and in operational performance. Some companies have built strong relationships with retailers in the UK. As it is evident that Irish firms cannot compete merely on price, two alternative strategies are suggested for future competitiveness:

- A strong combination of <u>design</u> and <u>marketing</u>. This would allow the firm to build a brand with a strong reputation.
- Strength in <u>service</u>, particularly in efficient turnaround of orders. This would allow the company to build a strength as a contract manufacturer.

In conclusion, a sectoral review commissioned by FAS (McIver Consultants, 1998), proposed the following vision of the industry:

"The vision should be of a knowledge-intensive industry that is strong on design, strong on marketing, strong on logistics management, strong on clothing technology.....and is positioned in markets where these strengths make sense. It could make reference to fashion and to branding. The vision would recognise that professional employment in the sector will increase, and that shop-floor employment may decrease."

REFERENCES

Kotler, P. (1994), *Marketing Management: Analysis, Planning, Implementation and Control,* Englewood Cliffs: Prentice Hall, 8th edition.

Euromonitor (1998), *European Marketing Data and Statistics,* London: Euromonitor Publications, 33rd edition.

Company Returns, The Companies Registration Office: Dublin.

McIver Consulting (1998), A Clothing Industry Update Study, report submitted to the Textile, Clothing and Footwear Committee and Fas: Dublin.

BIBLIOGRAPHY

Hollensen, S. (1998), *Global Marketing: A Market - Responsive Approach,* Hemel Hempstead: Prentice-Hall Europe.

Murray, J.A. and O'Driscoll, A. (1997), *Strategy and Process in Marketing,* Hemel Hempstead, Prentice Hall Europe.

www.fashion.net General source on fashion marketing and design.

www.jojomamanbebe.co.uk/ British mother and baby wear company.

www.formes.com French maternity wear.

www.valja.dk/ Danish maternity wear.

Koch, K. and MacGillivray, M.S. (1992), Information - based Data and Maternity Wear, *Journal of Home Economics:* Summer, 50-54.

Manley, J.W. and Cloud, R.M. (1993), Consumer Satisfaction with Available Selection For Those Who Wear Different Size Maternity Wear, *Journal of Consumer Satisfaction, Dissatisfaction and Complaining Behaviour,* Volume 6, 181-186.

Easey, M. (ed.) (1995), *Fashion Marketing,* London: Blackwell Science.

JUDY GREENE POTTERY[1]
MARKETING IRISH HANDCRAFTED PRODUCTS

Ann M Torres

"If at first you DO succeed, try something harder!"
Ann Landers, Syndicated Columnist

INTRODUCTION

Doing something harder is what Judy Greene has done and continues to do. In fact, Paul, Judy's husband and business partner, likens Judy to the blade on an ice-breaker ship. "Judy has to continually break the ice in developing new ideas. Judy never looks back; she is always looking ahead. Like most artists, her *next* piece is the most important."[2]

Judy Greene has established herself as one of the most prominent contemporary potters in Ireland. Her company, *Judy Greene Pottery*, is noted for the quality and design of its output as well as the entrepreneurial qualities of its director. Judy Greene is engaged not only in developing products and designs, but also in managing the manufacturing and retail operations of the firm. Judy's business has been successful, experiencing phenomenal growth rates over the last ten years. Her main concern is to ensure its future prosperity.

---

1 This case was prepared by Ann M. Torres, Marketing Department, NUI, Galway. It is intended to be used as a basis for class discussion rather than to illustrate either effective or ineffective handling of a business situation. The case is based on a real-life situation, but some figures are disguised.
2 Personal interview with Paul Fox, 25th August, 1998.

HISTORY OF *JUDY GREENE POTTERY*
& ASSOCIATED ENTERPRISES

Judy Greene Pottery

Prior to 1975, Judy Greene travelled considerably and made pottery everywhere from the Kalahari Desert to Switzerland. She learned different techniques and finishes which, later, she found very useful in bringing something new and varied to her business.

Judy Greene returned to Ireland in 1975 to manage *Potaireacht Cléire* (i.e. *Cape Clear Pottery*) located on Cape Clear Island, in West Cork. While there, she gained invaluable experience in managing and developing a thriving pottery operation. The realisation that she wanted to develop her own designs and break out of the style that characterised *Potaireacht Cléire* was the stimulus for her to go into business for herself.

In 1981, at 30 years of age, she decided she should start her own business. Judy had no capital when she started. She had no business plan and did not feel she had the time to take business-training classes. So, she put the key figures on a sheet of paper and went to see the bank manager. An overdraft of £15,000 was approved.

At that time, West Cork and Kilkenny were popular choices for potters, many of whom worked in small buildings out in the countryside and sold their product through retailers. Judy decided against this approach for two reasons. Firstly, she did not want to be limited to a three-month peak season each year that is typical for a tourist town. Secondly, she wanted to be in a position to receive regular feedback from the end customer, as she believed it would be an important influence on her design and product range in the long-term.

In 1982, she leased a small, 220 sq. ft. premises on Cross Street, in the centre of Galway City. With the aid of an IDA (Industrial Development Authority) capital grant, she purchased the necessary machinery and equipment. Her premises on Cross Street were to serve both as her workshop and retail outlet. Turnover in that first year of operation was about £14,000 which was enough for her to meet her rent (i.e. £6,000 per annum), her other overheads and to earn a frugal living.

Judy worked seven days a week for the first five years, staying overnight regularly to 'baby-sit' the kiln. In 1986, due to a longer recessionary period than expected, the business nearly folded. Determined to keep her doors open, Judy used her overdraft facility with the bank to advertise every holiday in the year (e.g. Halloween, Christmas, Valentine's Day etc.) Her investment in advertising paid off as turnover for that year approached £47,000.

It was in 1988 when Judy introduced the *Bluebell* line that she truly established and defined her style. Sales turnover for 1988 reached £96,000 and sales from the *Bluebell* range accounted for 60% to 65% of that year's turnover. Flowers and the natural landscape of Ireland were to become her design trademark and between 1988 and 1995 Judy introduced a new flower line every year.

Up until 1988, Judy worked as a sole trader; at that stage demand for her work was so great that she set up a limited company. Between 1988 and 1994 *Judy Greene Pottery* experienced exceptional growth and success, whereby the growth in sales volume doubled in every year. By 1994, sales turnover had reached £400,000. Judy attributes her success, in those years, to having her workshop on the retail site allowing for close, consistent contact with customers. In fact, customers were vital in providing feedback for testing new product ideas. Judy noted that, "if it worked it sold. The customers walking through the workshop were like having a marketing department walking through the door everyday."[3]

In response to her expanding enterprise, Paul Fox, Judy's husband joined the business in 1990, as general manager and financial controller. In 1992, Judy moved her workshop out of her retail shop and into a 4,000 sq. ft. IDA premises, on the outskirts of Galway City.

Design Concourse Ireland

Judy was consistently amazed by the array of talent of Irish designers, manufacturers and craftspeople. However, it struck her that the general public rarely had an opportunity to view these talents under one roof, as there were few venues for designers and craftspeople to display their wares. Hence,

---

3   Personal interview with Judy Greene, 20th February, 1998.

Design Concourse Ireland was born, which is a retail outlet offering a stunning range of handmade, Irish designed products such as jewellery, clothing, art, modern glass, furniture, and assorted home furnishings. It is set in a restored seventeenth century merchant's house in the medieval quarter of Galway, in Kirwan's Lane.

The Greene Corner
In 1996, Judy had a vacant retail shop next to her Cross Street premises. Her options were to lease it, or do something with it. So, she decided to open *The Greene Corner*. Her idea for this retail enterprise sprung from her interest in recycling and conservation of the natural environment. *The Greene Corner* offers a wide selection of goods made from recycled materials.

JUDY'S VISION
Currently, Judy is contemplating what to do next - a perplexing issue. As mentioned, her handmade pottery has been extraordinarily successful and she wishes to focus on developing future strategies to ensure continued prosperity. However, it can be challenging to develop successful strategies, particularly when everything is going well. Nevertheless, Judy is aware that the one thing she can count on is change. Consumer tastes tend to be cyclical. So, although pottery has enjoyed enormous popularity over the last ten years, Judy believes that in time other products (such as china and cut glass) will be favoured over pottery. Consequently, her company needs to be prepared to meet these changes.

Her vision for the future is to remain first and foremost a potter. With respect to new markets for her pottery, Judy is currently developing a line for the gourmet food/cookware sector. She believes that other sectors such as bathroom, lighting and aromatherapy/health (e.g. oil burners) still have further potential to tap. In addition, Judy identifies potential for specialised market niches such as the wedding gift market, where she believes there is plenty of room for innovation, and the corporate gift market for which special commissions may be executed. Another opportunity for product development lies with large corporations, such as *Waterford Crystal*, which in 1997 commissioned Judy's design expertise to develop a product based on *Waterford's Lismore* cut. In Judy's view, this marrying of corporate clout with designer skill has enormous potential for further development.

An essential objective is to develop the *Judy Greene* brand and to capitalise further on her strong brand presence. Her idea is to develop a number of value-added products, such as linen, glass, home accessories etc. under the *Judy Greene* brand. In this respect, even if potential customers were not interested in pottery per se, they would still be drawn to enter her retail shop. Furthermore, Judy believes there is an opportunity to expand the retail trade for the *Judy Greene* products. Her idea is to establish a group of outlets, distinctly branded as *Judy Greene* shops.

Furthermore, she would like to broaden her customer base. One way to achieve this is by developing her mail-order business which she currently does on a limited scale (i.e. usually at the request of a customer, but not via an established catalogue.) In terms of export markets, she believes the UK may be a promising market and she is considering whether to develop a presence in the US market.

Finally, Judy believes she will need to employ additional managerial staff if she is to achieve her vision. Among her three enterprises, Judy employs 22 people, but strategic planning is handled between Paul and Judy. Whilst Judy would like to give more time to marketing, as she feels it is one of her strengths, she also wants to retain a strong influence on design. Therefore, it is likely that the firm will need to recruit a marketer in the future. In addition, the manufacturing workshop would also benefit from the presence of a dedicated manager, as it is the nerve centre of the company and where a majority of the staff are located. In the long-term, it is likely that a managing director will be appointed who, with Judy and Paul, will play a key role in the firm's strategic developments.

STRATEGIC CHALLENGE

In 1997, following the establishment of *Design Concourse Ireland* and *The Greene Corner*, Judy focused on consolidating her core business - pottery. Sales volume for that year had reached £700,000. In 1998, sales volume rose an additional 15%. Judy's aim is to achieve £1,000,000 (+) in sales by the year 2000. By 2005, Judy would like to see an additional 25% growth in sales on the level achieved in the year 2000.

However, the question remains, what to do next to ensure future growth and success? She believes there are a number of issues to consider before developing and embarking on a development plan, such as the *Judy Greene* brand, competition, changing customer base etc.

It is interesting to reflect on the strengths and opportunities available to Judy's firm and to identify the strategic options facing the business at this stage. Inevitably, choices have to be made as resources will not allow Judy to do everything she has envisioned - at least not all at once. Judy believes her business is at a critical stage of development and certain key decisions will determine the firm's future strategic development.

IRISH MARKET FOR GIFTWARE AND CRAFTS

According to the Crafts Council of Ireland, "the Irish crafts industry has come a long way in the last 15 years because there has been a fundamental change in attitudes by craftspeople. They have recognised that succeeding is as much about running their business well as having a good product to sell."[4] As of 1998, the Irish crafts/gift market had an estimated annual turnover of £100 million (see Table 1.) Handcrafted pottery accounted for approximately 9% of that market. Depending on the product category, an average of 60% to 75% of this £100 million is attributed to the domestic market. Given that Ireland has a population of about 3.7 million,[5] per capita expenditure on Irish craft/gift goods is estimated to be between £16 and £20 per person. In the case of handcrafted pottery, the proportion of turnover attributed to the domestic market averages at 80%. Hence, per capita expenditure on pottery is less than £2.

---

4   Ibid.
5   Irish Central Statistics Office, 1998.

TABLE 1 - IRISH CRAFTS/GIFT MARKET FOR 1998

Sector by Product Category	**Est. Market Size in £m**
China, Porcelain, Stoneware Earthenware, & Tableware	16.75
Handcrafted Crystal & Glass	16.00
Handcrafted Pottery	8.75
Ornamental Giftware from China, Porcelain, Crystal & Glass	50.00
Studio Crafts (e.g. weaving, textiles, woodturning, wrought iron etc.)	8.50
Total	**100.00**

Sources: An Bord Tráchtála & Crafts Council of Ireland

Pottery made in a studio environment (i.e. handcrafted) has 70% of the Irish market, and is usually found at the upper price band for tableware and gift items.[6] Imports, mainly from the UK take the remaining 30%, but this percentage is expected to rise in the future. As handcrafted pottery is positioned in the upper price band of the market, it is not as price sensitive as other product categories. This is mainly attributed to the fact that original design, and strong customer preferences for design and colour protect pottery from competitive forces.

The craft/gift industry had been a growth market for many years. However, there are signs that growth is beginning to slow. Opportunities for the handcrafted pottery sector are in targeting specific consumer niches, such as:

• tableware for the "up-market" restaurant trade in Ireland;

---

6 *Market Opportunities - Giftware Market Republic of Ireland,* An Bord Tráchtála, based on estimates given in 1994 and calculated for 1998, pp. 6-7.

- development of complete tableware ranges for consumers;
- international "gourmet housewares" market - combining the unique method of production and use of material with functional design;
- European visitor who perceives Ireland as a country of rustic lifestyle and has a high level of awareness for craft products;
- corporate gift market, at home and abroad; and
- bridal and/or new home owners market in Ireland.

Pursuing some of these markets may stretch many potters' resource capabilities. Thus, to pursue some of these markets successfully, may require some automation, an option that is typically resisted by potters. Therefore, potters will need to select carefully those markets to which they believe their talents and resources are most appropriately matched.

There are several trends which relate to the Irish craft/gift industry overall:

- The young and more travelled customers are moving away from traditional and safe gifts. These types of customers are more influenced by international design trends and are attracted to innovative gift items.
- The influence from the tourist industry continues to be strong. However, the changing share and importance of the country of origin of the visitors will influence growth and design trends.
- The healthy economic climate provides a good foundation for opportunities not only for established firms, but also for new entrants. Thus, the industry is likely to become more competitive.

UK MARKET FOR GIFTWARE AND CRAFTS

The United Kingdom, being the nearest neighbour to Ireland, is often perceived as an attractive export market. However, the UK gift and craft market is characterised by immense fragmentation and variety. On the positive side, increases in disposable income, and in the size of upper-middle class socioeconomic categories (A, B, & C1), have contributed to growth in this sector. Hence, there is a market for higher priced, good quality products.

Opportunities for Irish craft manufacturers rely on meeting retailers' needs. For example, many UK retailers require differentiated products, and some require exclusivity. Currently, there are niche opportunities for handcrafted products in the quality gift sector. However, Irish craft manufacturers must be aware of their strengths in supplying a unique style or product and be adaptable in terms of customising their products for the UK market.

The types of outlets that are likely to be of interest to Irish craft manufacturers are:

- **Galleries** – which specialise in selling one-off or limited edition pieces;
- **Up-Market Gift Outlets** – which sell expensive hand-made or hand-fashioned items as well as established branded goods; and
- **Souvenir Outlets** – at major tourist attractions or located in major tourist centres such as Windsor, Oxford, York or Edinburgh.

The market in Britain is competitive. It is often difficult for new suppliers to establish a business relationship with retailers. An additional challenge for any Irish craft manufacturer is that UK retailers tend to buy from local sources as they prefer the convenience of a local supplier. This is particularly true in Scotland and Wales, which are more nationalistic than England. Up until the 1990's, awareness of Irish products and experience with Irish manufacturers was low. However, research has indicated that UK retailers have an extremely positive attitude towards sourcing from Ireland, if the products and suppliers can compete with alternatives in Britain.[7]

When dealing with "imported" products, many UK retailers prefer to deal with an agent, at least initially. Once a relationship has been established, most UK retailers will place orders directly with the craft manufacturer. The single most important source for information regarding new products is trade exhibitions, such as *Top Drawer* at the Olympia in London, and *The Spring Gift Fair* at the NEC in Birmingham. Additional sources for new products include, direct approaches by a manufacturer and observation of a product on display elsewhere.

---

7   Ibid.

The primary criteria in the selection of new products are exclusivity, originality, design and value for money.

As in the case of the Irish market, estimating the market size for handcrafted pottery is difficult. The population of the UK is about 58 million persons and estimates on per capita expenditure for handcrafted pottery vary. The low estimates show that UK per capita expenditure is roughly on par with the level in Ireland (i.e. about £2 per person.) While the high estimates show that UK per capita expenditure on handcrafted pottery may be twice the level in Ireland.[8]

Judy has previously tried to sell to the UK market, but her attempts were undermined by the long period of recession there.[9] For the first time, the firm has exhibited this year at *The Highlands Trade Fair*, in Aviemore, Scotland which Judy sees as the first serious step into the British market. However, to date, the sales are disappointing. This may be attributed, in part, to the lack of a local presence (i.e. agent) to promote and support her products. As a result, Judy believes she will need an agent/distributor who will enthusiastically "champion" *Judy Greene Pottery* in the UK. Still, she believes that "there is potential for selling pottery in Britain where all things Irish are currently in vogue."[10] Judy is further encouraged by the fact that "feedback from British retail customers during the tourist season in Galway has been consistently positive."[11]

US MARKET FOR GIFTWARE AND CRAFTS

The value of the US gift and craft market is estimated to be between $9 and $12 billion annually (i.e. IR£6 and IR£8 billion.) The market is immense, encompassing 50,000 to 70,000 different buyers for over 100,000 different retailers, many with

---

8 European Marketing Data and Statistics 1998, Euromonitor Plc., London, England. and *Tourist Opportunities in the UK for Irish Gift Manufacturers,* Bord Tráchtála, July 1998.

9 McGarry, Séan, "Appendix: Case Study - Judy Greene Pottery," *Business Manager 2000: A Guide to Building Your Business in the New Millennium,* Published by Bank of Ireland, 1998, p. 117.

10 Oliver, Emmet, *"Pottery Firm Plans Major Export Drive,"* The Irish Times, 6th of February, 1998.

11 McGarry, Séan, "Appendix: Case Study - Judy Greene Pottery," *Business Manager 2000: A Guide to Building Your Business in the New Millennium,* Published by Bank of Ireland, 1998, p. 117.

multiple locations.[12] Gift/craft merchandise is sold through various channels such as:
* Speciality Stores;
* Chain Stores;
* Catalogue Houses;
* Mass Merchants;
* Direct Response (e.g. mail-order and catalogues);
* TV Cable Network (i.e. TV shopping);
* Premiums and Incentives (e.g. gifts with purchase); and
* Department Stores.

Of these outlets, speciality stores are probably the most appropriate channel for Irish craft manufacturers. This is because speciality stores tend to operate on a smaller scale than the other channels and are very successful at selling one-of-a-kind and limited edition craft products. Furthermore, speciality stores work on building a personal relationship with customers, not usually provided in other retail outlets. In turn, speciality retailers look to their suppliers for in-depth product information and service.

The sources that US retailers rely on for buying products are primarily sales representatives and secondarily trade shows. Although trade shows in the US occur almost daily, the most important shows are in key markets such as New York, Los Angeles, Atlanta, Dallas, Chicago and San Francisco. The less predominant sources for purchasing include catalogues, telephone sales and showrooms.

The US gift retailer finds it difficult to survive on a narrow product assortment. Hence, gifts offered by retailers may range from men's neckties to aromatherapy candles. Consequently, the market is vast and products sought are wide in scope with many product sub-categories. The top ten product areas in the US gift and crafts market, are:
* Collectibles;
* Picture Frames;
* Tea, Teapots and Cups;
* Gourmet Foods and Accessories;
* Garden Accessories;

---

12 *US Gift Industry Handbook,* Enterprise Ireland, October 1998, p. 1.

- Decorative Accessories;
- Executive Gifts;
- Plush Items (i.e. at the collectible end);
- Greeting Cards and Stationery; and
- Aromatherapy Items.

Opportunities for handcrafted pottery may be found in developing products suitable for any of the above gift categories. For example, with respect to garden accessories, popular products are indoor-desk fountains, bird houses, bird baths, watering cans, and row markers (i.e. name plates to identify plant.) For the aromatherapy gift market, there is a demand for ceramic/pottery oil burners, baskets and decorative containers designed for potpourri, candles, essential oils and other aromatherapy products. In terms of gourmet foods and teas, there is demand for suitable accessories such as ceramic/pottery honey pots, olive plates, serving dishes, teapots, cups and other traditional delph items.

Research suggests that a typical US consumer spends about $20 on gifts (i.e. about IR£13.33) in an average month (i.e. not for Christmas.)[13] Some US consumers, classified as 'collectors,' spend about $30 (i.e. IR£20) on gifts in an average month.[14] Given that the population of the US is about 272 million, the average monthly expenditure on gifts is substantial.[15] However, accurately estimating the proportion of expenditure attributed to pottery is problematic. This is because the US gift market is segmented into thematic product categories, such as the ones shown above (e.g. gourmet foods.) Hence, segmentation is not drawn according to the type of product material (e.g. crystal, china/porcelain, pottery, etc.)

SOURCES OF COMPETITION AND COMPETITIVE POSITIONING

Judy Greene Pottery has several sources of competition; the stiffest emanating from:
- Irish (handmade) luxury gift products, such as modern glass, wooden bowls, wrought iron etc., which are close product substitutes for handmade pottery.

---

13 Ibid., p. 1.
14 Ibid.
15 US Department of Commerce, Bureau of the Census, April 1999.

- Imported luxury gift products of Eastern European origin (e.g. Poland, Hungary, Czech etc.) where labour costs and product prices are low. Many of these products have flooded the market, thus lowering the price and profit for domestically produced items.
- Traditional china, porcelain and cut glass markets (e.g. Royal Tara China, Waterford Crystal etc.) which are regaining popularity.

The most obvious source of competition is from other Irish potters. To a certain extent, other Irish potters are not the fiercest source of competition for *Judy Greene Pottery*. Most potters stay within distinct colours, shapes and designs that have become their trademark. Given that every potter has a unique, distinctive style that becomes their brand identity, when choosing a brand of pottery, customers usually find one, perhaps two brands, immediately more attractive than others. Therefore, once the decision for purchasing pottery is made, the choice of the brand of pottery is not as complex. Although, given the healthy economic climate, there is a bloom of new Irish potters coming on to the market who are successfully attracting the younger customers with their designs. In addition, there is a general expectation of increased competition from imported brands of pottery.

It is difficult to estimate accurately the market share of individual potters (see Table 2.) This is because most enterprises are privately held, owner/manager operations, that run on a very small scale of 1 to 3 persons. According to the Crafts Council of Ireland, there are about 255 potters registered with them, most of whom operate on a very small scale. Currently, there is no distinct market leader, as many of the potters who run larger operations are on a relatively equal standing in terms of reputation, market share etc. There are six potteries of a similar size to *Judy Greene Pottery* around the country and they network regularly, exchanging information on a variety of things, but on design in particular. These six potters are:

- ***Nicholas Mosse*** (Bennets Bridge) - has the largest operation of all the Irish potters and enjoys a healthy export market to the US and the UK. *Nicholas Mosse Pottery* is known for its traditional folk spongeware designs and is a popular range which customers often ask for by name. In addition, the firm offers a wide range of value added products (e.g. table cloths, napkins, lampshades etc.)

- **Louis Mulcahy** (Dingle and Dublin) - is considered to be a "potter's potter." He has a good presence in Ireland and currently exports some product to Europe. Most of his sales are made through his three retail shops located in Dingle, Ballyferriter, and Dublin and through major retailers (e.g. *Meadows & Byrne* and *In-Store*.) Currently, he is the single biggest employer on the Dingle peninsula.

- **Stephen Pearce** (East Cork) - is perhaps the most prestigious of the Irish potters. He offers several ranges of pottery that he sells in Ireland and exports to the US. In addition to his pottery interests, he is involved in design and architecture.

- **Michael Kennedy** (Sligo and Gort) - has been based in Sligo for years and has recently opened a second manufacturing workshop and retail shop in Gort. His designs produced in Gort avail of salt glazing techniques, which are strikingly different from his line produced in Sligo. He also exports some of his products to Europe.

- **Michael Jackson** (Bennets Bridge) - produces *Stoneware Jackson* and is one of the few potters to avail of a brand-name other than his own name. He runs a large workshop in Bennets Bridge and a small retail shop in Kilkenny.

- **Suzanne May** (Dublin) - runs her workshop and small retail shop in the IDA Centre on Pearse Street in Dublin. She is actively pursing the Scottish and English markets.

TABLE 2 - ESTIMATED MARKET SHARE OF
HANDCRAFTED POTTERS FOR THE IRISH MARKET
FOR 1998

Potter	Est. Market Share
Nicholas Mosse	16%
Louis Mulchay	14%
Stephen Pearce	12%
Judy Greene	8%
Michael Kennedy	6%
Michael Jackson (i.e. Stoneware Jackson)	5%
Suzanne May	5%
Other Potters (i.e. small operations of 1-3 persons)	4%
Total Sales for Irish Handcrafted Pottery in Ireland	**70%**
Total Sales from Imports (e.g. UK, France etc.)	30%
Total Sales for Handcrafted Pottery in Ireland	**100%**

Sources: Judy Greene Pottery, Crafts Council of Ireland & Craft Society of Ireland.

It is true that most potters are artists or craftspeople first and business people second. Typically, they are late to develop the business infrastructure for their operations. This is where Judy may have an edge over other Irish potters. She counts among her strengths her ability to deliver innovative designs, coupled with a good business sense.

CUSTOMER PROFILE AND SEGMENTATION

Judy's current customers are mostly female, 25 to 45 years of age and older, coming from mostly middle and upper middle incomes. Many of the younger customers (i.e. mid-twenties to mid-thirties) are newly married couples and/or new homeowners. Segmentation of her customers is given in Table 3 and shows that the domestic market takes the lion share of sales. From April to September, sales to foreign markets increase. Tourists buy in the retail shop and ship their purchases home, perhaps purchasing again later through mail-order. Most of these tourist/mail-order sales are made to customers from the US (90%); smaller proportions are made to tourists from the UK (5%), and other countries (5%). Export sales are made through individual retailers who have sought out *Judy Greene* products or through supplying specialist consumer catalogues. The majority of sales are made to retailers in the US (55%); and smaller proportions are made to retailers from Canada (15%), France (10%), UK (10%) and other countries (10%).

TABLE 3 - CUSTOMER SEGMENTATION FOR *JUDY GREENE POTTERY* FOR 1998

Market Segment	Oct. - March	April- Sept.
Domestic	90%	80%
Export	2%	5%
Tourist	4%	10%
Mail-Order	4%	5%
Total	**100%**	**100%**

Source: Judy Greene Pottery

CHANGING CUSTOMER TRENDS

Another issue is Judy's expectation that customer tastes will change. Pottery, in general, has been very fashionable for the last ten years. The china, porcelain and cut glass (i.e. crystal) markets have suffered at the expense of natural, earthy designs. Customer trends are changing and their tastes appear to be moving slowly away from pottery back to china, porcelain and cut glass. Most important for Judy is to identify and stay ahead of the trends.

To identify future trends, Judy 'devours' interior design magazines and travels abroad to Europe and the United States to see what is popular and selling there. "Typically what is selling in Frankfurt now, will be in Ireland in 2 years time."[16] For this reason, she finds that the timing of new products and designs is crucial. In fact, the idea for one of her best selling products, oil burners, was developed as a direct result of a trip to a ceramics fair in Munich, 5 years ago. While in Germany, she went to numerous chemist shops to examine the design, function and safety features of various kinds of oil burners. It was one of the most cost efficient ways to do her R&D work. Thus, when she returned to Galway she wasted little time and resources in developing her final product.

Judy readily admits that reading interior design magazines and examining other markets is no guarantee of success in the Irish market, as design and colour trends may not suit Irish tastes. However, identifying the potential trends and then customising them for the consumers in the home market affords a better chance of success. Judy also relies quite heavily on customer feedback. The retailers and customers who buy *Judy Greene Pottery* are always looking for new designs, so Judy has to stay fresh and respond to their feedback. Judy is aware that she needs to capitalise on ideas for new lines to "stay fresh" in a highly competitive market. Yet, at the same time, she also knows that it is important to stay true to her own style. Balancing these two concerns is challenging while trying to satisfy customer demand.

With respect to design preferences, 10 years ago when Judy started, flowers and flowery designs were 'in.' Now, she has to consider what the upcoming generations want, as they will be the customers of the future. The younger age groups are more interested in simpler, more classical lines of design. Judy believes that "younger customers are looking for something Irish, but not hackneyed symbols of shamrocks and shillelaghs." In response, Judy introduced her *Connemara Collection* to appeal to the younger markets. In addition, Judy introduced her limited edition, *Millennium Line* to appeal to the more sophisticated tastes of an older market. The *Millennium* pieces are once-off or limited production designs that will be unavailable after the year 2000.

Furthermore, Galway being a tourist town, there are the

---

16 Personal interview with Judy Greene, 10th August, 1998.

tastes of visitors to consider. Judy has noticed that the English tourists love the flowery designs and will buy everything in the shop. German visitors prefer the simpler designs and buy the larger, exclusive, unique and one-of-a-kind pottery pieces. The American visitors will be one of two types: either ones that buy "seconds" from the bargain baskets; or ones who buy entire dinner sets, because they like the design and consider money to be no object. Finally, the French and Italian tourists do not buy a lot of pottery and prefer to purchase items in *Design Concourse Ireland.*

As a member of the Galway Chamber of Commerce, Judy does have access to a research report, *Galway Tourism 1997*, which the Chamber of Commerce commissioned. According to this report, there were 920,000 visitors to Galway City in 1996 (see Table 4). These visitors stayed an average of 3.5 days in the city and spent an average of £60 per day. Typically, for every £1 spent by tourists in Galway City, only £0.08 was spent on gifts.

TABLE 4 - VISITORS TO GALWAY CITY FOR 1996

Country	Percentage
Ireland & N. Ireland (i.e. other than Galway)	42%
United Kingdom	17%
United States of America	15%
Germany	8%
France	7%
Other Europe	7%
Rest of World	4%
Total	**100%**

Source: Galway Chamber of Commerce

FOCUS GROUP RESEARCH

Although Judy believed she had a good understanding of her loyal customers, she thought it worthwhile to investigate various other (potential) customer segments. Her objectives in pursuing this research were to learn more about:

- Where people got their ideas for fashion, interior design and home furnishings?
- What were their general perceptions of porcelain, china, and pottery?
- What brands of pottery did they know, like, and buy (i.e. for themselves or a gift)?
- What were their buying patterns and criteria when buying pottery?

Judy was interested in qualitative information that explained why people think or feel the way they do and so hired a market research firm to organise and facilitate focus group interviews. The researchers identified four customer types to interview and the findings from these interviews are summarised in Appendix A. A broad profile of each type is given below:

- *Young Graduates* – are in their early- to mid-twenties. They have just finished their undergraduate studies, and in the process of postgraduate studies, or in their first job. They represent future customers. In time, they will be homeowners, and perhaps (loyal) future *Judy Greene* customers.

- *Professionals* – are in their early-thirties to mid-forties. They are homeowners and professional women. They represent customers with higher disposable income.

- *Homemakers* – are in their mid-forties to mid-sixties. They may be women who identify themselves as homemakers, or who work part-time outside the home, or who are retired. They represent the mature customer who has had a home for a number of years, and for which she has purchased numerous items.

- *Loyal Customers* – are of various ages, in various stages of their life cycle, and of any occupation. The only criterion is that they are loyal *Judy Greene* customers.

PRODUCT

Flowers and the natural landscape of Ireland are *Judy Greene's* design trademark. The *Bluebell* line, introduced in 1988, established her brand identity. Subsequent to the *Bluebell* range and up until 1995, she developed a new flower range every year, evocative of the natural environment around her. During 1996, Judy consolidated her design lines and brought out new products (e.g. honey pots, jam jars, and kitchen accessories etc.)

The *Connemara Collection*, which Judy brought out in 1997, was aimed at younger customers. It was a departure in that it was not a flower. However, the abstract designs incorporating heather blues, forest greens and natural, earthy tones still captured the essence of the natural landscapes of Ireland. In the same year, Judy introduced her limited edition *Millennium* line. Like the *Connemara Collection*, this line is a departure from her trademark of flowery designs. The attraction of the *Millennium* line lies in the shapes and contours of the products, as well as the simplicity of design, which avails of a green marbleised glaze over a terracotta base. Due to the higher price, Judy expects the *Millennium* range to have a limited appeal, mainly to an older audience.

During 1998, Judy developed a range of gourmet cookware products. These products have a very different look from the highly glazed and decorated *Judy Greene* trademark of flower and landscape designs. Essentially, she has produced a range of basic pottery that is reminiscent of the "old farm house" look (i.e. plain terracotta with a transparent glaze.) The advantage of these products is that they open another market for *Judy Greene Pottery*, the food market. In addition, production of this gourmet cookware requires no R&D work, as she is using existing resources and capabilities.

A further advantage to the gourmet cookware line is that she may be able to link it to a range of food products and mixes. Judy has had initial talks with Susan Slevin, who runs *Irish Village Traditional Food Mixes* (e.g. Traditional Brown Soda Bread Mix, Tea and Breakfast Scones Mix, Porter Cake Mix) and who is successfully exporting her food products to the US. Through the work of an excellent agent, Susan Slevin has an established customer base in a number of up-market, gourmet food shops and department stores. The target US consumers for these food mixes are the health conscious, those looking for convenience, the ethnic Irish market abroad, and the tourist market. The idea is that, when Susan is merchandising, demonstrating and/or sampling her products, using *Judy Greene* cookware, she will develop the potential for sales of, and a customer base for, *Judy Greene Pottery* in the US.

RETAIL STRUCTURE AND DISTRIBUTION

Handcrafted products within the Republic of Ireland are sold direct from the source to the retailer. Only imported products are sold through wholesale companies. Typically, handcrafted pottery has a limited distribution in speciality shops (e.g. *Meadows and Byrne, In-Store* etc.) and gift shops (e.g. *Blarney Woollen Mills, House of Ireland, Treasure Chest* in Galway etc.) This is partly due to the limited availability of pottery products, but also due to the exclusivity demand from strong retailers. The exception to this is imports, which are mainly distributed through the department stores (e.g. *Brown Thomas, Debenhams* etc.)

Although most of *Judy Greene* pottery (i.e. 60%) is sold through Judy's own retail shop, she does sell through other retail outlets. Judy's distribution to speciality and gift stores is outlined in Table 5. Presently, she is in the process of scaling back on the number of retailers she supplies, from 150 to 120 shops. Most of this reduction has been made in the area of very small accounts. The reason Judy gives for pursuing this strategy is to eliminate very low profit accounts, to give superior service and support to the larger, more profitable accounts, and to increase the exclusivity of her product. Judy has noticed a similar trend among other potters and, consequently, sales are becoming more regionalised. Thus, Judy finds that most of her retail sales are in Galway and the west; *Stephen Pearce* is most strongly entrenched in Cork and the south-west; *Michael Kennedy* sells to Sligo, Gort and the north-west etc.

TABLE 5 - RETAIL OUTLETS SELLING
JUDY GREENE POTTERY

Type of Retail Outlet	Estimated No.	% of Retail Outlet
Large	42	35%
Medium	36	30%
Small	42	35%
Total	**120**	**100%**

Source: Judy Greene Pottery.

Retail buyers in the speciality and gift shops constantly review their existing product ranges on offer in their shops. Typically, they are open to new products and suppliers, if a retail buyer can demonstrate a unique proposition. Design quality and depth of product range are fundamental requirements for a new range to interest retail buyers, who believe that too much of the same type of product is not in the best interests of their customers. Thus, shelf space is not easily given to new products at the expense of already established products and brands. The criteria most important to these buyers, are design differentiation, (very high priority), depth of product range, guarantee of continuity of supply, price and value for money.

All retail buyers use trade fairs to source new products and to review product developments from existing sources. The most frequented trade shows are "Showcase" in Dublin for Irish made products; the "Spring Fair" at NEC Birmingham in the UK, as well as Frankfurt and Milan for internationally sourced products. There is a trend among gift shops, which used to stock mainly Irish-made products, to stock an increasing number of non-Irish products. The reason for this may lie in the greater profit margins these retailers can place on imported products. Retailers' standard mark-up on wholesale prices for Irish handcrafted pottery is low, usually between 2.1 and 2.2 times the wholesale price. Whereas, mark-up on imported products may be substantially higher, perhaps double or triple the rate for Irish products.

PRICING

Handcrafted pottery is not as price sensitive as other sectors in the craft industry. This is mainly because it is perceived as a labour intensive product and thus the price is accepted - within reason. In addition, the leading brands of imports (e.g. *Denby Pottery* and *Poole Pottery*) are positioned at the upper end of the market and, as such, set price expectations. Pricing among the major potteries in Ireland is rather stable. All the major potteries have relatively the same pricing structure. The standard mark-up for retail prices is 2.1 to 2.2 times the wholesale price. Thus, Judy's own retail shop sells *Judy Greene* products at the same retail price as other retailers.

Judy Greene Pottery, like the other major potters, aim their product at the middle and upper income markets. Pottery is usually sold as giftware and is not typically sold in sets. Thus, the retail price points range from £8, for a small item, such as a mug, to £200 for a large item, such as a lamp. The greatest volume of sales is made in the £9.95 to £29.95 retail price range. Average retail price points for gift items, such as wedding gifts is higher at £40 to £50. Table 6 outlines the retail price range and average retail price for various pottery items.

TABLE 6 - AVERAGE RETAIL PRICING FOR HAND-CRAFTED POTTERY

Product Type	Price Range	Ave. Retail Price	*Judy Greene's* Price
Dinner Plate	£12 - 26	£15.00	£16.95
Mug	£8 - 12	£8.50	£8.50
Small Bowl	£7 - 15	£9.00	£9.50
Small Vase	£5 - 12	£8.00	£9.95

Sources: An Bord Tráchtála, Crafts Council of Ireland, & Judy Greene Pottery

Judy Greene Brand - Tangibilising the Intangible

In the case of pottery, typically the potter's name becomes the brand. Each potter has a unique, individual style that develops into his/her distinct brand identity. *Judy Greene*, as a brand, is strong and well established in Ireland. To a certain extent, the *Judy Greene* brand is a paradox. Some customers perceive the firm as being a big, multinational with massive operations like those of Waterford Crystal. While others, think of it as being manufactured in the back kitchen of a cottage.

Judy believes the qualities that the *Judy Greene* brand communicates most strongly are: handmade and hand painted, quality, exclusivity, light, natural, earthy, flowers and natural landscapes of Ireland, and Irish without being trite. An issue remains as to how to develop this concept and communicate it to retailers and customers successfully, thereby enhancing the brand further and without diluting its value as an asset. In the past, customers looked for products that were "too perfect" to be handmade. Now, customers understand that handmade products will not be identical and appreciate variations as part of the crafted product.

Judy wants to continue to communicate and tangibilise the handmade aspect to customers. She believes that the increased use of point of purchase information and signage, throughout the retail store may be useful. This is because Judy has noticed that although the outdoor signage says *Judy Greene Pottery*, consumers are not aware that the products in the store are mainly *Judy Greene* products. Other ideas include giving tours of her manufacturing operations, and placing a potter's wheel in her retail shop to give demonstrations. Still, Judy considers there may be other things she could do to tangibilise her handmade products.

PROMOTION

The most typical promotional tools used in the craft industry are product leaflets and information cards on the crafting of the product. A new initiative which Judy and other potters have pursued (i.e. *Louis Mulcahy, Michael Kennedy, Suzanne May, Kiltrea Bridge,* and *Etain Hickey*) is investing in "combi-ads," whereby a number of potters collectively buy full-page advertising. Although there is considerable effort in organising these ads there are dramatic savings on expenditure. Judy spends about 4% to 5% of her turnover on promotion. Table 7 outlines the allocation of her budget to various promotional efforts and their ranking in order of importance.

TABLE 7 - *JUDY GREENE POTTERY* PROMOTIONAL BUDGET ALLOCATION FOR 1998

Promotional Tool	% of Budget	Rank in order of Importance
Brochures	7%	1
Bags, Tags, Packaging	7%	2
Merchandising & Window Displays	1%	2
Ads in Interior Design Magazines	38%	3
Ads in Tourist Magazines	25%	3
Ads in Local Newspapers	20%	3
Misc., Once-off expenditures	2%	4
Total	**100%**	

Source: Judy Greene Pottery

Judy believes that her best promotional investment was in developing her brand identity. In 1992, she spent £12,500 to overhaul her brand and to develop a more professional, modern, brand image. She commissioned an Italian design firm to develop the *Judy Greene* brand mark that would appear on everything from the brochures, to the delivery van. Judy is aware that a brand's image and identity should be up-dated periodically. She believes that the most opportune time to have done this was in 1996. Unfortunately, that was at the time when *Design Concourse Ireland* and *The Greene Corner* had opened and there was little cash to invest in marketing. Hence, she believes revising the brand is an issue that merits priority.

WHAT NEXT?

Although *Judy Greene Pottery* is currently a successful venture, Judy wants to ensure the firm's future profitability. She has many issues to consider in developing a long-term strategy to achieve her vision. Among them are growth, and the level of growth to pursue in domestic and export markets. Furthermore, she is interested in developing ways to capitalise on the strength of the *Judy Greene* brand. Creating new product lines, incorporating value added products, and establishing retail shops under the *Judy Greene* label are some options that could advance the brand. With respect to the Irish market, she must evaluate customers in terms of their changing profile and preferences. Competition is always a relevant issue, and Judy recognises that new, as well as well established potters, may affect her positioning. Naturally, these decisions will affect the product, its pricing, distribution and promotion. What advice would you give Judy Greene in developing her long-term strategy to fulfil her vision?

APPENDIX A: FOCUS GROUP INTERVIEWS

SUMMARY OF FINDINGS FROM FOCUS GROUP INTERVIEWS

The focus group interviews were disguised. Thus, *Judy Greene* was not identified as the research client. The facilitator followed a list of questions to guide the general direction of discussion, but the setting was informal to ensure the conversation flowed easily. The findings from the focus group interviews are summarised on the following pages.

Young Graduates – Future Customers

The average age of participants in this focus group was 23 years. All participants had finished their undergraduate studies. At the time of the interviews, they were in the process of postgraduate studies, or in their first job. None of them owned their own home, and were either living in the family home, or in rented accommodation.

The *Young Graduates* described themselves as being very style and fashion conscious. They were very aware of current fashion trends. In addition, many of them liked to buy branded products and perceived that a good brand name added value to their purchases. Most of their influences came from magazines, shop windows, or their peers. However, they also had a clear idea of what they liked and the designs and styles they preferred.

Professionals – Higher Disposable Income Customers

The average age of participants in this focus group was 36 years. All participants were homeowners and professional women in a full-time job. The majority of these women were married and had children.

The *Professionals* viewed themselves as very practical individuals who preferred comfort, convenience and simplicity in their surroundings and clothing. Terms such as "very convenient, no thought involved, easy to manage and maintain, comfortable and practical," were mentioned frequently as important factors for purchases to suit their lifestyle. Many of the *Professionals* said that they led busy, hectic lives and sought purchases that made their lives easier.

Homemakers – Mature Customers

The average age of participants in this focus group was 50 years and they had their home for a number of years. Many of the women identified themselves as homemakers, even though many of them work outside the home, or did so at one time. All the women were married and the majority had children.

The *Homemakers* felt that words such as "casual, functional, traditional and classical" most accurately described themselves and their preferred surroundings. Influences on their choice of style came from themselves, magazines, as well as their friends and relatives. However, they did not believe they were influenced by trends in fashion. Essentially, they had developed their own style and preferred to "stick with it."

Loyal Customers – Core Customer Base

The fourth focus group was composed of loyal *Judy Greene* customers. As this was the only criterion, participants' profiles were more diverse than in the other focus groups. The women ranged in age from 35 to 67 years. All the women had their own home. Most of them were married and many of them had children. Half of the participants were professional women in full-time positions, and they ranged in age from 37 to 54 years. The other half identified themselves as homemakers, and they ranged in age from 35 to 67 years.

The *Loyal Customers* perceived themselves to be independent thinkers. They did not believe they were heavily influenced by trends in fashion and interior design. In general, they favoured clothing and home furnishings that were: "classical, elegant, and of good quality." Although they appreciated classical styling, they did not view themselves as traditional. Consequently, they clarified that they preferred "an old style with a modern twist, and a mix of antique and modern furnishings." Essentially, they liked "things that won't date, that are smart, but not too trendy." Many of these women expressed an opinion that "fashion was for younger people." Essentially, they felt they were at a stage in their lives where their identities were established and they were comfortable with themselves.

As a whole, the groups preferred pottery to china and porcelain. Still, each group did have distinct characteristics in terms of motivation for purchase, importance of branding, purchase criteria, and preferences for style, design, colour etc. Appendix Tables 1 and 2 summarise the participants' responses from the focus group interviews

APPENDIX TABLE 1 – SUMMARY OF CUSTOMER PROFILES

FOCUS GROUPS:	Young Graduates	Professionals	Homemakers	Loyal Customers
Customer Segment	Future Customers	High Disposable Income Customers	Mature Customers	Core Customer Base
Description of Personal Style	"Classical Casuals"	"Practical Minimalist"	"Functional Traditionalist"	"Timeless Modernist"
Purchase Motivations	Brand, style and current trends	Convenience, practicality, functionality, and value	Function, personal taste, & habit (Not by brand & fashion.)	Quality, function, consistent w/own styles – i.e. timeless, smart, won't date
Perception of Current Fashion	Retro, 50's style, tailored, classical casual	Space, efficiency, functionality, bright, airy, timeless, simplistic, minimalist	Natural, wood & earth tones, changes slowly over time	Country style, spacious, airy, more for younger people
Pottery Preferred (i.e. with respect to style, design, colour etc.)	Simpler, less fussy designs, in bold colours and shapes – like a lot of variety	Clean, simple lines, in white, natural and terracotta tones	Traditional (terracotta) designs & lines in muted colours	Classical lines with a modern twist, but timeless

APPENDIX TABLE 2 -
SUMMARY OF FOCUS GROUP FINDINGS

FOCUS GROUPS:	Young Graduates	Professionals	Homemakers	Loyal Customers
Q1: Where do you get ideas for fashion, interior design & home furnishings?	Magazines, peers, shop windows, self, "what I like"	Magazines, peers, friends, i.e. what others did in their homes	Magazines, out of own head, friends and relatives	Irish Magazines, visit the shops, own style
Q2: How do you describe your own style and that of your surroundings (i.e. home or accommodation)	Own style is casual, easy to maintain, comfortable; style brand & quality conscious, very fashion conscious & very aware of trends	Practical, comfortable, focused, minimalist, simple, convenient, consistent	Casual, functional, individualistic, not overly concerned about fashion	Classical, good quality, elegant, independent thinkers, smart styles, not too trendy or dated,old-style w/ a modern twist
Q3: Words you associate with china and porcelain?	Formal, dainty, dust-collectors, old-fashioned, out-of-date	Too out-dated, costly, expensive, fussy, delicate, irritating	Dainty, impractical, unused, flowery, expensive, not for everyday	Delicate, lovely, pretty, formal dining room, formal, never used
Q4: Words you associate with pottery?	Earthy, natural, raw/unaffected, in fashion	Functional, chunky, durable heavy,	Chunky, practical, functional, old-fashioned	Warm, earthy, comforting, casual, intimate
Q5: What are important factors when buying pottery?	Colour, shape, design, texture, depends on occasion	Occasion, (gift) recipient's taste & preferences, look & design, function, & price	Practicality, functional, shape, colour, simplicity, design, style	Shape, colour, functionality
Q6: What brands of pottery are you most familiar with (i.e. name recognition)?	*Stephen Pearce, Judy Greene,* and to lesser extent *Nicholas Mosse , Michael Kennedy*	*Stephen Pearce, Judy Greene* and to a lesser extent *Nicholas Mosse*	*Stephen Pearce, Judy Greene* and *Nicholas Mosse*	*Stephen Pearce, Jack O'Patsy, Judy Greene, Louis Mulcahy & Nicholas Mosse*
Q7: How important is the brand (name) in general & when purchasing pottery?	Very brand and style conscious.	Brand not a big issue – more emphasis on function, convenience, comfort & price-value relationship	Brand name is not important	Appreciate value of brand, but brand name is more important for gifts
Q8: How important is price when purchasing pottery?	Brand carries (a lot) more importance, but they also look at price carefully	Value conscious more than price conscious	Price is not very important	Price is not at all important
Q9: How important is in-store service?	Very important	Convenience is very important	Important part of the purchase experience	Extremely important

APPENDIX B: ADVERTISEMENTS FOR JUDY GREENE POTTERY AND COMPETITORS

Home Thrown

Louis Mulcahy

Judy Greene

Suzanne May

Michael Kennedy

Kiltrea Bridge Pottery

Etain Hickey

• Barkers, Wexford • Blarney Woollen Mills • • Bricin, Killarney •
• Design Concourse Ireland, Galway • Design Options, Portlaoise •
• Erin Country Knits, Kenmare/Sneem • Instore, Limerick • Judy Greene, Galway •
• Michael Kennedy, Sligo & Gort • The Kilkenny Shop, Dublin • Kilkenny Design, Kilkenny •
• Kiltrea Pottery, Enniscorthy • Suzanne May, Pearse St. IDA, Dublin • Meadows & Byrne, Cork •
• Louis Mulcahy, Ballyferriter/Dingle/Dublin • Quinlans, Macroom • Rossmore Studio, Clonakilty •

Home Thrown

Louis Mulcahy, Ballyferriter/Dingle/Dublin • Kilkenny Shop Dublin • Blarney Woollen Mills •
• Bricin, Killarney • Design Concourse Ireland, Galway • Design Options, Portlaoise •
• Judy Greene, Galway • Instore, Limerick • Whichcraft, Dublin • Erin Country Knits, Kenmare/Sneem
• Michael Kennedy Sligo & Gort • Kilkenny Design, Kilkenny • Meadows & Byrne, Cork •
• Kiltrea Bridge, Enniscorthy • Quinlan's Macroom • Barkers, Wexford • Bridge Gallery, Dublin

Judy Greene Pottery
Cross Street, Galway,
Ireland
Tel: (091) 561753
Fax: (091) 770008

Greene Pastures

Judy Greene has moulded a lucrative niche for herself in the pottery business.

Report by Geoff Percival

RETAILING AT DUBLIN AIRPORT – A GROWTH STRATEGY FOR THE NEW MILLENNIUM

Mary Wilcox

INTRODUCTION

Mr. Stephen Duffy, Marketing Manager for Dublin Airport's retailing outlets, was on his way to meet with his marketing team. As he strode through Dublin's bustling terminal his thoughts were racing: Aer Rianta's profits up 15 per cent to £52.3 million in 1998; sales at the Dublin Duty Free up 20% to IR£82 million - fantastic! A decision to float Aer Rianta now seemed certain. *Compact* being implemented. Lots of change on the way. Proposed abolition of intra-EU duty-free was the big fly in the ointment: £30 million lost off bottom line profits was a lot to make up. Not just up to Dublin's marketing team, but Aer Rianta's Dublin flagship store as the group's biggest and best business unit must lead the way. What a challenge! Still, all the options were on the table, choosing the right way to go was the trick. Over-night change would be impossible. Repositioning and redefining a business was a long-haul process - not for the feeble-hearted - with multiple issues: pricing, merchandise mix, outlet location, promotion, customer culture. The Icelanders were a live example of international marketing. Stephen swung open the door of the meeting room and greeted his team.

AN INTERNATIONAL MARKETING CHALLENGE

The Icelanders are an interesting example of pure shopping and, in theory, Dublin Duty Free was ideally placed to market its offerings to them. These visitors, who rarely stay longer than a few days, come to Dublin to shop. They spend on average £1,500 per head in downtown stores, but the spend in duty-free is a tiny fraction of that figure. What is wrong? Why don't they shop in duty-free? Why don't they buy? Take alcohol as an example. In Iceland, very few stores sell liquor, and those that do sell it at an exorbitant price. In Dublin Airport, a bottle of whiskey costs half the down-town Dublin price and still the Icelanders don't buy. Icelanders have one of the lowest rates of alcohol consumption in the world. Is this because there is a lack of supply, because of price, are there legal restrictions on what can be brought into the country or is it purely a cultural phenomenon?

How to entice Icelandic shoppers (and other non-EU passengers) to spend more at Dublin Duty Free is the key question. Even in the area of tax-free products, the airport is performing below its potential. Part of the problem may lie with the powerful influence that shopping tour guides have in choosing shopping destinations, but crowded airports have eroded discretionary time (dwell time), and the risk perceived in deferring shopping until the last hour compounds the situation. On arrival, passengers off the Icelandic flight are targeted with duty-free shopping brochures that develop an awareness of the potential of shopping in duty-free prior to boarding. Although they are in Dublin Airport two hours before their return flight, various processes reduce dwell time. Checking-in and a 'tax-back' cash-refund facility provided by a commercial organization eat into the time available for duty-free shopping. (Queueing for the tax-back facility can take anything up to forty minutes). Part of the problem may be that Icelandic passengers may fear that what they are looking for may not be available at the airport. Part of the marketing challenge is to make sure that the product is there and secondly to reinforce that message through promotion and advertising at the airport. There may be a problem in delivering value to the Icelandic customer in the sense that the merchandise-mix is not what the Icelanders want. Dublin Duty Free is lacking in a number of leading brands – Rolex, Diesel, Barbour jackets and so forth. These are the products the Icelanders seem to be buying, but Dublin Duty Free doesn't actually sell them.

AER RIANTA

Aer Rianta has recently achieved a new status. It is no longer merely an agent of the Government but is a fully commercial semi-state company responsible for managing Ireland's three

State airports and associated activities. The company now has control of all its assets and will be liable to pay corporation tax and rates. Options for the future of Aer Rianta include the continuance of the status quo, privatization, a strategic partnership or flotation. A consultant's report now with the Government is thought to advise some form of flotation. The company is in the process of implementing *Compact for Constructive Participation*, a joint company/union initiative that emphasises partnership and flexibility.

Aer Rianta's primary objective is to provide safe and efficient facilities and services at the three airports at the lowest possible cost to airlines and passengers. The company is profitable and growing and all indicators are positive. (See Appendix A, for a 1997 five-year financial summary, Appendix B, for a 1997 five year ratio analysis and Appendix C, for 1997 passenger traffic statistics). 1998 was a record year for passengers with a total of 14.8 million using the airports at Dublin, Shannon and Cork, an increase of 11% over 1997. Dublin Airport handled an additional 1.3 million passengers. Traffic for the first quarter of 1999 is growing at unprecedented levels, averaging growth rates of 20% at each of the three airports. The company attributes this success to growth in the economy, the maintenance of very competitive access costs and the introduction of new route networks. Twenty-three airlines now use Dublin Airport providing services to sixty-one scheduled destinations. Aer Rianta is currently carrying out a comprehensive review of its airport charges which have not been increased since 1987. The chairman, Mr. Noel Hanlon, puts forward the view that the current level of airport charges does not provide an economic return on the capital expenditure requirements for developing the three airports. However, Ryanair, one of Ireland's biggest airlines, constantly complains about the level of Aer Rianta charges and has flown a kite about the possibility of opening a second airport at Casement Aerodrome.

Capital investment spend at Dublin Airport between 1990 and 1996 averaged IR£16 million per annum. A major capital investment programme is now underway, with forecast capital expenditure at Dublin Airport between 1998 and 2001 set to reach IR£275 million. The duty-free shopping area has doubled and the final improvements will bring the capacity of Dublin Airport to

20 million passengers, and serve passenger and airline needs with the most up-to-date facilities and improved customer service standards. Although in 1999, 20,000 car spaces will be available at Dublin Airport, at peak time demand can barely be met.

Aer Rianta has a long history of involvement in the duty-free business and can claim to have invented the concept by opening the world's first airport duty-free shop at Shannon in 1947. Dublin Airport's duty-free retailing is the Group's most profitable business unit and the company's flagship store. In 1998 the three Irish duty and tax-free shops continued to perform exceptionally well with sales revenue amounting to £105 million. The proposed abolition of intra-EU duty and tax-free sales in June 1999 will have a significant effect on Aer Rianta's cashflow and profitability and the company has lobbied strenuously against its abolition. Most of its revenue derives from the sale of duty-free goods. Initially abolition was to take place in 1992, so a seven-year deferral gave the company time to prepare. In 1988 "Aerofirst", a joint venture company set up by Aer Rianta and the Soviet airline, Aeroflot, opened new duty-free shopping facilities at Moscow Airport. The success of this venture inspired Aer Rianta to set up a subsidiary, Aer Rianta International (ARI), to develop commercial ventures both within Russia and in countries in Europe, Asia and the Middle East. ARI has the management contract for the duty-free shops at Eurotunnel, one of the largest duty-free operations in Europe. Although the volume of sales reached record levels in the Eurotunnel operation, ARI's contract with Eurotunnel expires in 1999. The collapse of the Russian economy affected duty-free in Moscow and St. Petersburg. In 1998 ARI invested IR£9.45 million in acquiring the concession for seven duty-free shops in Canada, its first duty-free venture in North America. All of ARI commercial activities are either joint ventures or management contracts. Capitalizing on the trend towards airport privatization worldwide, ARI bought into airports in Birmingham and Dusseldorf, both of which are performing beyond expectation. Other business interests include eight Great Southern Hotels and in 1998 the company established Property as a separate business division with the mandate to develop a property portfolio. The Group is now engaged in the development of a business and technology park at Cork Airport. During 1998 the

Group divested itself of its US mail order business and its interest in Aer Rianta Bewley Ltd.

RETAILING AT DUBLIN AIRPORT: A CHANGING BUSINESS

For Aer Rianta, duty-free retailing at Dublin Airport is a very successful 'associated commercial activity' and Dublin Duty Free is the largest earner in the Group. Up to June 1999, departing passengers could expect to save approximately fifty per cent on whiskey and maybe sixty per cent on cigarettes as against average UK/Irish downtown prices. In addition to tobacco and liquor, the outlet also offers a good selection of tax-free branded products. As and from 1st July 1999, if the abolition occurs, the intra-EU tax-free side of the business will disappear and the company will join other retailers in a Value Added Tax (VAT) scenario. Aer Rianta will pay VAT on the cost price of goods and pass on a charge of twenty-one per cent VAT to customers. However, for some time to come, the company may still have a price advantage. In addition to being VAT-free, duty-free shops are also excise-free. Informed sources all indicate that duty-free outlets will continue to be excise-free for a period of two and a half years. The amount of excise charged varies by product category, for example, the element of excise on perfume is very small, only a few percent, but on the average bottle of whiskey the excise approximately equates to thirty per cent of downtown price and nearer to forty per cent for tobacco.

Although there are no planning regulations to restrict it, landside retailing (retailing outside of the boarding areas) has not developed in Irish airports. Two reasons contribute to this phenomenon – seventy per cent of Aer Rianta travellers are either domestic or UK passengers, both of whom have a strong duty-free culture. The second reason is even more cogent – increased passenger numbers have put space at a premium. Dublin Airport has fewer landside retail outlets now than it had four years ago because the physical dynamics of moving passengers has to take precedence.

SUPPLIER ARRANGEMENTS

Duty-free is a worldwide industry and companies that supply this industry distinguish between the duty-free and duty-paid market. Suppliers have two separate divisions with different departments, different people, and different negotiation strategies for duty-free and duty-paid. This is so for tobacco and liquor and for most leading duty-free brands. Aer Rianta undertakes a form of collaborative buying, as opposed to centralized in the conventional sense of the word. While other retailers, e.g. Tesco, have centralized control in every sense of the word, Aer Rianta doesn't have this. However, there is close collaboration on issues pertaining to price negotiation with suppliers. While there has been an element of polarisation in supply sources, generally the duty-free market is supplier driven; suppliers come up with concepts, sometimes in collaboration with the retailer, but the main impetus is often from the supplier. Own-label brands have been considered, but no decisions have yet been taken.

MERCHANDISE SELECTION

Liquor and tobacco form an important part of the merchandise offer and are strategically positioned within the store. An 'exclusive to duty-free' range of products was conceptualised by some of the spirit companies and Dublin Airport sells some exclusive whiskey products but the general offer is available downtown, at double the price. In Aer Rianta's duty-free outlets, the selection of merchandise has evolved on an historical basis, e.g. blue-chip products such as *Waterford Crystal* and other major brands must be stocked to meet the demand of the tourist market. As the Group's most proftable business unit, the Dublin store has the widest product range and grouping. The recent successful addition of a *Manchester United Shop* to Dublin's offer was supplier driven, but the denim store which is targeted at the younger traveller and stocks both *Levi* and *Wrangler*, is an Aer Rianta concept. At the moment, signage within duty-free is disrupted because on-going physical developments render signage out of date every two weeks. Space constraints also affect decisions on concession offers. At the moment about fifteen per cent of turnover comes from concessions. In 1990/91 the company introduced scanning for duty free goods and a system is now being developed for tax-free goods. This technology speeded the check-out operations and helped with stock control but had little impact on merchandise range.

PRICING STRATEGY

Aer Rianta has a deliberate policy of pitching their price below most UK operators and is happy that customers have a positive price perception, certainly for liquor and tobacco. Management occasionally spot-check prices downtown, and respond to negative feedback on prices. For example, via special offers, some downtown stores were undercutting tax-free prices for jeans, which led to Aer Rianta taking lots of fire on pricing structure. The company reacted in a very positive way from the customer's point of view, reducing prices substantially (and hence margins) to maintain competitiveness. But even duty-free shops could never compete with some markets, e.g. in the US, Levi 501s cost $24.

PROMOTIONS

In-store relevant promotions and brochures themed around events are used to target specific groups of travellers, specific markets, e.g. Americans arriving for St. Patrick's Day, rugby groups, and so on. More general day-to-day and point-of-sale promotions are used to boost sales. Within the last few years, advertising themes have become a little daring, not quite what would normally be associated with a semi-state company. One particular advertisement used a skunk to highlight the desirability of purchasing perfume at Dublin Duty Free with the copy: 'Who forgot to get their perfume at Dublin's Duty Free?' The advertising is designed to have mass appeal to the travelling public. Eighty to ninety percent of advertising resources are concentrated on tax-free products such as electronics, suntan lotions, gifts of all descriptions, rather than duty-free products. Media buy tends to focus on billboards, but radio has been used and 1998 was the first time a press campaign was used. Research subsequently recorded the highest ever advertisement awareness levels. The campaign featured a 'Famous Names Significantly Reduced' theme that was thought to be better suited to a press campaign (Appendix D). The theme was used flexibly in different publications, e.g. when buying space in the likes of *Image* magazine, a skin-care product was the focus.

MARKET RESEARCH

Dublin Duty Free conducts both qualitative and quantitative research. The qualitative research is undertaken by a specialist organisation and focus groups are drawn from a passenger mix. In addition to demographic profiles, the marketing team has a knowledge of markets by country of residency, e.g. purpose of travel and what people's perceptions of duty-free are. Do they have a duty-free culture? Do they like duty-free shopping? For example, using a Likert rating scale, subjects were asked to respond to the statement: 'I really enjoy browsing in duty-free shops.' Respondents were then categorised by residency, e.g. Irish, UK citizens, European mainland, and North American residents. That particular question yielded the information that mainland Europeans and Americans browse a lot less than their UK and Irish counterparts. Other research uncovered the information that both Europeans and Americans buy less, with Americans buying the least. Dublin Retailing also has information on who buys what, e.g. one in every ten passengers buy perfume and of those who buy, sixty per cent are Irish. Gender differences have been identified – e.g. women enjoy browsing and shopping more than men do.

If contemplating introducing a new product category, e.g. a new range of leather goods or introducing computer software products, "we would look to market research to validate whether we are going in the right direction or not. In other words, we try to get some feedback from customers as to whether they would purchase such a range if we were to list them in our range of products in Dublin Airport."

About sixty per cent of passengers make a purchase in Dublin Duty Free. The nature of the purchase varies between different merchandise grouping, cigarettes and liquor sales are higher, perfumes and tax-free gifts less so. Airports measure market share, or market penetration, by the number of transactions divided into the number of passengers. However, because one passenger could arguably constitute three transactions, it is reasonable to assume that the penetration rate is somewhat over-stated.

Dublin Duty Free has made many in-store changes based on feedback from market research. Four years ago, negative feedback on congestion, product location, accessibility to retail outlets, the general tiredness of the retail offer and an absence of quality customer care prompted management to invest in revamping and refurbishing the stores. Follow-up research has shown that customers appreciated the changes. The extent of customer satisfaction is measured in a quantitative survey carried out once yearly at a peak and non-peak time. Most rating factors have shown significant improvement, e.g. value for money, product range and layout of shops. Helpfulness of staff has shown some improvement, but despite training programmes, customer- care programmes and quality management programmes, there is still a long way to go. Staff incentives focus on sales commission and prospects of promotion, which are somewhat limited. The duty-free shops have a slow rate of staff turnover, and some staff, supervisory and others, have been in place for more than twenty-five years.

UK DATA

- During the early 1990s, despite the recession that affected UK high street retailers, airport retailing boomed.

- Total retail sales at UK airports rose from £380 million in 1989, to £550 million in 1993, an increase of 45% (Corporate Intelligence, 1994).

- For specialist shops (i.e. those which are not duty-and tax-free) the rise in sales has been more spectacular – an increase of 220% (from £25 million in 1989 to £870 million in 1993).

- In 1993/4, British Airport Authority (BAA), whose airports account for 80 per cent of the UK market, reported that 42.6 per cent of its turnover came from rental income from its retail concessions (Retail Verdict, 1995).

- Many retailers have experienced exceptionally good sales per square foot in airport shops, compared with similar outlets on the high streets. Bookshops in London's Heathrow and Gatwick airports are achieving sales of between £2,400 and £1,800 per square foot (BAA plc and Corporate Intelligence 1994).

- Sales densities at Bally's Heathrow Airport shops are the

highest in any of its UK outlets: between £2,300 and £2,600 per square foot. (Corporate Intelligence, 1994)

• The average spend per passenger is estimated at £6.40 (Daily Telegraph 12 Jan. 1994).

• London Heathrow and Gatwick airports currently attract many internationally known retailers such as Harrods, Liberty and Bally, as well as specialist retailers.

• Findings from Baron and Wass's research found that responsdents (83 per cent) looked around the airport shops. Some seventy-five per cent of the total respondents bought from the airport shops. However, only fifty-seven per cent admitted to associating airports with shopping.

• Those who do make the association are more likely to browse and make a purchase in airport shops.

• In a survey of 1,984 *domestic* airport passengers in the USA, Butler and Jernigan (1993) concluded that air passengers had a low propensity to shop in the airport shops and generally experienced low levels of satisfaction with the merchandise on offer. The main purchases were 'reading materials and candy or other edibles.'

• The airport which provided the setting for the research paper regards retailing as a vital contributor to revenue and the aim is to increase commercial income by five per cent more than the increase in passenger throughput.

Appendix A					
FIVE YEAR SUMMARY OF FINANCIAL RESULTS					
	1997 IR£000	1996 IR£000	1995 IR£000	1994 IR£000	1993 IR£000
TURNOVER					
Dublin Airport	122,593	109,286	104,178	92,295	79,005
Shannon Airport	68,251	69,412	58,713	54,615	56,939
Cork Airport	12,260	11,633	10,509	8,938	7,874
Subsidiary and other business activities	43,693	40,976	39,109	38,342	31,583
Total	246,797	231,307	212,509	194,190	175,401

CONTRIBUTION BY AREA					
Airports					
Dublin - **Operations**	14,361	13,350	12,737	10,159	9,887
- Commercial	28,443	24,500	20,852	17,211	12,685
- Total	42,804	37,580	33,589	27,370	22,572
Shannon - **Operations**	834	501	1,166	1,451	2,463
- Commercial	1,745	1,874	1,442	1,056	1,864
- Total	2,579	2,375	2,608	2,507	4,327
Cork - **Operations**	81	(83)	116	(517)	(237)
- Commercial	2,983	2,487	2,052	1,644	1,279
- Total	3,064	2,404	2,168	1,127	1,042
Subsidiary and other business activities	10,762	9,639	7,161	8,126	3,711
Central costs, Aer Rianta Technical Consultants and other costs not allocated to business units	(13,665)	(9,886)	(7,971)	(8,001)	(8,975)
Profit before taxation	45,544	42,382	37,555	31,129	22,677
Taxation	(3,802)	(3,376)	(3,557)	(3,888)	(2,092)
Minority interest	308	406	57	411	0
GROUP PROFIT FOR THE FINANCIAL YEAR	42,050	39,412	34,055	27,652	20,585
Profit expressed in constant 1997 prices (Consumer Price Index applied)	42,050	39,987	35,134	29,244	22,284

Appendix B					
FIVE YEAR RATIO ANALYSIS					
	1997	1996	1995	1994	1993
Profitability					
Return on average capital employed	20.2%	22.7%	23.6%	23.6%	22.0%
Return on average investment	14.6%	17.0%	17.6%	17.1%	15.7%
Profit margin	16.9%	16.7%	16.1%	15.2%	14.3%
Efficiency					
Average asset turn	0.8	0.9	0.9	1.0	1.0
Employee costs to turnover	27.7%	26.9%	26.6%	28.5%	29.6%
Liquidity					
Current ratio	0.6	1.2	1.0	0.8	0.6
Quick ratio	0.4	1.0	0.8	0.7	0.5
Gearing					
Debt/Equity	46.2%	2.4%	18.3%	29.9%	43.3%
Interest cover	24.0	26.5	15.7	11.4	5.8

Definitions

Return on average capital employed	Profit before interest, taxation and minority interest divided by the average of fixed and net current assets/liabilities.
Return on average investment	Profit before interest, taxation and minority interest divided by the average of fixed and current assets.
Profit margin	Operating profit divided by turnover.
Average asset turn	Turnover divided by the average of fixed and current assets.
Employee costs to turnover	Payroll and related costs divided by turnover.
Current ratio	Current assets divided by current liabilities.
Quick ratio	Current assets less stocks divided by current liabilities.
Debt/Equity	Debt, net of cash, divided by capital and reserves.
Interest cover	Profit before interest, taxation and minority interest divided by the interest charge.

Appendix C					
FIVE YEAR SUMMARY OF TRAFFIC STATISTICS					
	1997	1996	1995	1994	1993

PASSENGERS					
Overall					
Transatlantic	1,032,166	991,300	866,464	829,918	708,601
Great Britain	7,614,919	6,789,638	5,864,923	5,000,251	4,276,950
Europe	3,261,279	2,884,820	2,641,078	2,304,924	2,005,690
Domestic	850,465	804,873	751,836	654,939	630,364
Transit	592,698	485,635	443,297	525,571	749,744
Total	13,351,527	11,956,266	10,567,598	9,315,603	8,371,349
Dublin					
Transatlantic	535,078	477,881	401,550	397,656	316,721
Great Britain	6,361,256	5,624,094	4,897,760	4,185,817	3,502,469
Europe	2,850,287	2,454,181	2,249,564	1,973,801	1,730,712
Domestic	488,017	464,510	434,079	369,158	355,261
Transit	98,564	70,630	41,941	54,551	32,963
Total	10,333,202	9,091,296	8,024,894	6,980,983	5,938,126
Shannon					
Transatlantic	496,947	512,271	464,831	432,149	391,802
Great Britain	496,137	467,151	376,762	331,165	339,502
Europe	192,906	214,756	207,702	187,817	156,878
Domestic	157,431	145,256	129,254	117,674	114,466
Transit	478,643	401,216	392,836	465,627	707,333
Total	1,822,064	1,740,650	1,571,385	1,534,432	1,709,981
Cork					
Transatlantic	141	1,148	83	113	78
Great Britain	757,526	698,393	590,401	483,269	434,979
Europe	218,086	215,883	183,812	143,306	118,100
Domestic	205,017	195,107	188,503	168,107	160,637
Transit	15,491	13,789	8,520	5,393	9,448
Total	1,196,261	1,124,320	971,391	800,188	723,242

TERMINAL FREIGHT incl. MAIL (Metric Tonnes)					
Dublin	122,619	107,004	86,401	72,655	65,292
Shannon	39,497	35,463	34,026	29,314	26,315
Cork	8,095	4,214	3,717	2,294	2,502
Total	170,211	146,681	124,144	104,263	94,109

APPENDIX D

swatch

Famous Names.
Significantly Reduced.

Famous Names. Significantly Reduced.

Repositioning Eircell and Building a Valuable Brand

Patricia Medcalf

TRANSFORMING EIRCELL INTO A VALUABLE BRAND

INTRODUCTION

It is Autumn 1995 and Stephen Brewer has recently been appointed Chief Executive of Eircell. Challenging times lie ahead, with the Irish mobile phone market poised to reap the benefits of a sector that continues to grow faster in Europe than any other business. Brewer has experienced similar situations before when working in senior management positions with France Telecom in France and Cellnet in the UK. In both cases, he played a key role in steering these companies successfully through radical change, and it was these credentials which made him the ideal leader for Eircell.

When he arrived, Brewer selected a new senior management team and appointed one of Ireland's specialists in corporate identity, The Identity Business. Together they would work to devise and implement a change programme which would bring all of Eircell's stakeholders into the next phase of the company's development. Today he was chairing a meeting where various members of the team (including him) would present their best thinking as to how the company should proceed.

BACKGROUND - THE FIRST ELEVEN YEARS

Eircell was launched in December 1985 as a division within Telecom Eireann. It was positioned as a luxury business service at a time when mobile phones cost £4,000. Coverage was primarily in the Dublin/Leinster area, and for the next 11 years Eircell would enjoy monopoly status. This gave them the opportunity to single-handedly develop the Irish mobile telephony market.

TABLE 1 CUSTOMER PROFILE 1985-92

Phase 1 Chief Executives, Directors
Phase 2 Sales forces, technical support services
Phase 3 Small to medium sized businesses who need to be in contact with their customers and suppliers on a continuous basis. They included plumbers, electricians, doctors, vets, local emergency services.

Between 1985 and 1992, Eircell invested heavily in its 088 analogue network. It also developed relationships with a number of independent mobile phone retailers who attempted to promote the concept of one-stop shopping to the customer. In order to make phones more affordable for the end customer, commission payments were given to these agents to enable them to reduce prices for different models.

In June 1993, Eircell launched its 087 digital network which was built on Global Systems Mobile (GSM) technology. The GSM digital service has certain advantages, the most important being that it provides better call quality. It also allows the user to 'roam' i.e. to use the service in those countries, which have agreements with Eircell. It provides a platform for the development of value added services such as data and fax transmission. When launched, the 087 service was initially targeted at international business travellers.

By June 1995, the market was on the verge of moving from being the preserve of the business market to enjoying mass market appeal. Eircell introduced a new service in order to attract the non-business user. It was aptly called 'Eircell Personal', and it was offered on the 088 network. It consisted of an all-in-one package, which included a number of minutes of call-time. While Eircell Personal increased Eircell's growth rates, market penetration levels were lower in comparison with other countries.

KEY STRATEGIC ISSUES FACING EIRCELL AT THE END OF 1995

Without doubt, Eircell had reached a defining moment in its short history. Internal and external events were signalling strongly that the time for change had arrived.

1. Eircell was about to become a statutory limited company. This meant that by the middle of 1996 Eircell would be autonomous from its parent, Telecom Eireann, while at the same time enjoying the benefits of being associated with a giant of Ireland's corporate landscape.

2. Eircell's monopoly status would finally end in 1996 when one new operating license would be granted, followed by a second license to another player by 1999. For the first time the increasingly sophisticated mobile customer would enjoy choice. Those new to mobile communications would seek out the best deal on offer, while superior customer service would become an important aspect when selecting a service provider.

3. By the autumn of 1995 Eircell had in excess of 120,000 customers and 200 agents nation-wide. Trends in other markets around the world were pointing towards a transformation in the market from being a business only market to being a mass market. Indications were that the same phenomenon was about to occur in Ireland, and Eircell was beginning to enjoy accelerated growth in both their business and consumer markets.

The writing was on the wall. Pressure was mounting for Eircell to become more customer focused and to lose its staid, semi-state image.

FEEDBACK FROM KEY STAKEHOLDERS
Eircell conducted in-depth interviews with customers, staff, agents and business partners. A number of issues were uncovered, which would have to be addressed immediately:

- There was dissatisfaction with the quality and coverage of the network. Many customers frequently experienced call breakdowns and/or blackspots where they were unable to make any calls at all. For business users, these weaknesses were particular cause for concern.
- Agents and customers were concerned about the length of time it took between signing up with Eircell and being able

to make and receive calls. Customers wanted to be able to make calls as soon as they acquired the necessary apparatus.

- Agents and customers were confused about which leaflets contained the relevant information - this often resulted in the customer signing up for an inappropriate package.
- There was a tendency to overuse telecommunications jargon in all literature. In 1995 target users were not yet familiar with terms such as coverage, roaming, and analogue VS digital.
- Agents and customers were often unsure as to which application form they should use and agents were annoyed that they had to photocopy the completed application form twice - the original went to Eircell, one copy was given to the customer, and the agent also retained a copy for their own files.
- There was inadequate support for agents in terms of point of sale material. This made it difficult for them to attract and impress potential customers.
- Customers and agents were frustrated at the length of time it took customer services staff to respond to calls. This weakness was seen as particularly intolerable due to the fact that Eircell was a communications company.

A NEW VISION FOR A NEW ERA

Taking on board the information gleaned from the qualitative research, Brewer put in place a roadmap for the company which was embodied in a new mission statement for Eircell: *"to make Eircell the cellular network of choice in Ireland and to be famous for doing the right things well."* It was intended that this statement would serve as a clear signal for staff as they went about their daily tasks, whether they were interfacing with colleagues, agents or customers.

Brewer also wanted *"to make owning and using mobile phones more attractive and more affordable for as many people as possible. We aim to enable every Irish household to have access to a mobile phone."* His ambitions also included the need *"to transform Eircell into the most famous brand in Ireland and to ensure that the brand is synonymous with mobile communications."*

To clearly signal senior management's intent to staff,

agents, customers and the competition, Eircell recognised the need for a new brand identity. Brenda Moriarty, Head of Marketing, saw it as a *"catalyst for organisation change which would make our vision tangible for staff. We also want an identity system, which would result in time and cost efficiencies as well as a greater level of professionalism. With the arrival of competition, we have to make it easier for our agents to sell their services, thus giving us a competitive edge."*

POSITIONING PLATFORM

Based on the new mission statement, Eircell's new Chief Executive and his senior management team established three core values, which would form the basis of their positioning strategy. It would be vital to shake off any negative connotations such as staid and semi-state, unresponsive, and inefficient. Therefore it was intended that the new core values would underpin all of Eircell's activities. From now on everything they would do for staff, customers, agents, partners, suppliers and opinion leaders would have to reflect their new values, and enable Eircell to satisfy customers' needs for coverage, choice and care. The core values were:

1. Reliable

This meant that Eircell's remit must be to create a faultless network offering coverage, quality and capacity to the user. Eircell openly committed to building Ireland's biggest and best network through the deployment of a £120 million investment. The network was to be supported by an Integrated Customer Care System (ICCS) to handle all customer enquiries. A commitment was therefore being made to connect customers instantly to the network and in order to facilitate this, Eircell promised to fully support their agents.

2. Progressive

Eircell wanted to become an industry standard setter and this would mean being confident innovators without using customers as guinea pigs. Brewer intended stressing to staff the importance of being "famous for doing the right things well." Therefore Eircell would commit to offering customers the widest and best choice of packages in Ireland.

3. In-touch

This meant that Eircell must be committed to listening to customers, agents, staff and business partners. Staff would be expected to anticipate and exceed customers' requirements and needs. In practical terms, this would require them to communicate their services without resorting to jargon and complex application procedures. Eircell would also commit to finding out what customers wanted from them. Since agents and staff were an important link with customers, programmes would be implemented to keep them fully informed of campaigns and future plans.

A NEW BRAND IDENTITY

It was now the turn of The Identity Business to present a brand identity solution which would meet the objectives set out in the design brief:

* To communicate change to Eircell's various audiences;
* To clearly differentiate Eircell from the competition;
* To create an image of openness and accessibility ;
* To ensure maximum visibility in the retail environment.

In meeting the brief, The Identity Business conducted a visual audit, which involved gathering all of Eircell's current and past materials (e.g. sales brochures, advertisements, sponsorship material, stationery), as well as similar items from international mobile phone companies, equipment manufacturers, excellent service companies, and domestic and international agents. This very important exercise revealed that many mobile phone companies operating on the international landscape were very formal in their approach. Their visual identities communicated engineering excellence but said little about their affinity with customers. Colours used tended to be blues and blacks, and therefore it was difficult to distinguish between many of the companies. Most companies used upper-case lettering in their name. The Identity Business concluded therefore, that it would be very important for Eircell to be seen as approachable, and colour would be an important ingredient in the quest to attract and maintain attention.

The Identity Business also presented their findings on

Eircell's name, and whether or not it should change. As a result of the visual audit, and qualitative research, Eircell were strongly advised to retain their name. It was well-known, legally registered, and communicated the company's Irishness.

Eircell's brand mark was created to be the cornerstone of their corporate identity and should be seen as the primary expression of their values and personality. It was to be interpreted as follows:

- The focal point of the brand mark is the arc. It forms a smile, which represents the very heart of all communication - the need to talk.
- It creates an image of openness and accessibility and symbolises the dynamic, exciting future of telecommunications.
- The corporate colours, purple and blue were chosen to ensure maximum visibility and communicate the energy and vibrancy of the revitalised Eircell.
- The name Eircell was rendered in a lower case typeface so as to appear less formal and the 'r' was in a Celtic style so as to retain the company's Irish origins.

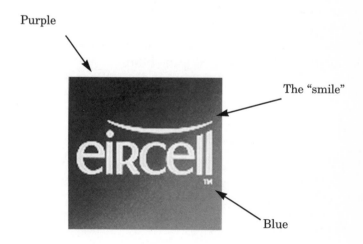

Brenda Moriarty supported this rationale by stating that the logo *"portrays openness, accessibility, warmth and friendliness."*

MEETING THE CHALLENGES

Stephen Brewer surveyed the room with satisfaction. Following today's meeting, he felt confident that the foundations had been laid for the next phase of Eircell's development. He had reaffirmed the mission statement, and core values, while The Identity Business had presented a visual manifestation of the company's vision. The meeting was concluded asking the following questions:

Question 1

How should Eircell launch the new brand identity to its key stakeholders?

Question 2

Following the launch, what type of integrated marketing communications programme should be devised in order to ensure the successful development of the Eircell brand? What role can the new brand identity play in introducing efficiencies?

Question 3

What type of product development programme should be implemented in order to stay ahead of the competition?

A follow-up meeting was scheduled when solutions to the above challenges would be presented.

APPENDIX 1 – INFRASTRUCTURE: NETWORK BUILD FIGURES 1994/96

TABLE 2

Number of base stations	December 1994	December 1995	% increase 1994-5	December 1996	% increase 1995-6
Digital (GSM)	125	204	63	354	75
Analogue	117	154	32	212	38
Number of cells					
Digital (GSM)	170	314	85	507	61
Analogue	205	269	31	358	33
Number of voice channels					
Digital (GSM)	1650	3100	88	7175	131
Analogue	3757	4996	33	7009	40

APPENDIX 2 - THE MOBILE PHONE MARKET IN IRELAND

TABLE 3
Mobile phone users January 1994 to January 1998

	1994/95	1995/96	1996/97	1997/98
Eircell	88,000	158,000	288,000	400,000
Esat Digifone				110,000

Source: Eircell

TABLE 4
Market penetration and market growth rates in the mobile telephony (actual and projected)

	Market penetration	Market growth
1996/97	8.7%	
1997/98	15.7%	
1998/99	22.3%	42%
1999/2000	27.7%	24%
2000/2001	32.0%	16%
2001/2002	35.9%	12%
2002/2003	39.1%	9%

Source: Eircell

SLENDERTONE
CREATING A WORLD-CLASS BRAND

Michael J. Murphy

INTRODUCTION

Local auctioneer, Eamonn McBride, still remembers clearly the day in 1990 when Kevin McDonnell arrived in the truck in Bunbeg: "Kevin had asked me to organise accommodation for some employees of a new business he was setting up. I went to look for him on the industrial estate. I found him outside the factory in a big truck . He pointed to the equipment in the back of the truck and said, 'That's it there', referring to his new business. I was totally stunned." McDonnell had bought the remaining assets of a company called BMR, which had gone into liquidation. The deal included ownership of the company's brand names, 'NeuroTech' and 'Slendertone'. McDonnell had decided, against the advice of many, to re-establish the business in an old factory on the industrial estate outside Bunbeg. Bunbeg is a remote, windswept, coastal village in the Gaeltacht (Irish speaking) region of North-west Donegal. Within a few weeks McDonnell and five employees had begun production.

McDonnell says that he knew little about the business he was getting into when he loaded the truck in Shannon and drove north to Donegal. An accountant by training, he thought that, on paper, it seemed like a viable business. He now employs over 150 people in Ireland, and another 70 in international subsidiaries of his company, BioMedical Research Ltd. Company revenue in 1998 was £22 million[1] - £17m. of which was from sales of Slendertone, up nearly 60% on the previous year. The company has received a number of design, export and enterprise awards: McDonnell was voted 'Donegal Businessman of the Year' in 1995. But McDonnell has little

---

1 Some of the figures, names and other information given in this case have been altered to protect company and customer confidentiality. However, all data given is representative of the actual position.

time or desire to reflect on his substantial achievements to date. Not while he has still to attain one of his greatest goals: to develop Slendertone into a world-class brand.

McDonnell believes Slendertone can be a £100m a year business by the year 2002. He likes to relate how Slendertone now outsells popular brands like 'Impulse' and 'Diet Pepsi' in the UK; or how Slendertone is now available in Selfridges, the prestigious department store in London. McDonnell is under little illusion about the arduous challenge that lies ahead. However, he believes he has the strategy to achieve his goal. He is confident that the recent marketing strategy devised by Brian O'Donohoe will enable Slendertone to achieve sales of over £100m in two years and to become a world-class brand. O'Donohoe, now managing director of Slendertone, joined the company as marketing director for Slendertone in April 1997.

According to O'Donohoe, "BioMedical Research as gone from being a product-oriented company to a market-led one." In the process O'Donohoe has had to identify and deal with a number of critical issues. He believes that the foremost issue facing the Slendertone brand is credibility. He stresses the need to get away from the 'gadget' image associated with Slendertone. O'Donohoe is confident that his strategy to re-position the Slendertone brand will successfully resolve this issue. Product credibility is one of a number of important issues to have arisen since Slendertone's creation over thirty years ago. O'Donohoe knows the future of Slendertone as a world-class brand depends on how well his strategy deals with these and other issues which have arisen more recently, due to the company's dramatic growth.

SLENDERTONE: THE EARLY YEARS

Slendertone was originally developed by a company called BMR Ltd. in 1966. The company moved from England to the tax-free zone in Shannon in 1968. BMR manufactured a range of Electronic Muscle Stimulation (EMS) devices under the Slendertone[2] and NeuroTech brands, serving the cosmetic and medical markets respectively. By the end of the 1980s BMR's

---

2 This case study focuses on the Slendertone division. Readers who are not familiar with EMS, or Slendertone, are advised to read the appendix (What is Slendertone?) before proceeding with the case.

total annual sales were £1.5m. Around 40% of revenue was coming from the sale of NeuroTech products, used by medical practitioners and physiotherapists to treat conditions such as muscle atrophy. The balance came from sales of Slendertone, used mostly for cosmetic purposes. 95% of Slendertone sales were to the professional (beauty salon) market with the remaining 5% coming from a limited range of home-use products. The home-use units were very basic, and had few features. They retailed for between £250 and £400. Margins on all products were high. BMR claimed that Slendertone was available in over 40 countries by the late 1980s. All international sales were being handled by small local distributors, or companies with diverse product interests (these included an oil importer and a garden-furniture dealer!).

Kevin McDonnell was a creditor of BMR at the time of its liquidation; he had been supplying the company with printed circuit boards for four years. In this time he had learned something about the company's operations. When he heard BMR was going into liquidation he immediately saw an opportunity. In an interview with the Financial Times in 1995 he stated: "I thought it was a bit odd that the company could go out of business and yet, according to its business plan, it was capable of a 20% return on turnover." Few shared McDonnell's belief in the future of the Slendertone business. The managing director of BMR's German office felt that Slendertone was a 'fad' which had little future.

McDonnell was not deterred. By the end of 1990 he had notched up sales of £1.4m, producing and selling much of the original BMR product range. With his focus initially on production, McDonnell continued to sell most of his products through distributors, many of whom had previously worked with BMR. Over the next two years revenue grew gradually through increasing sales to distributors of the existing product range. McDonnell re-invested all his earnings in the business. Research into bio-medical technology, with a view to developing new products, consumed much of McDonnell's limited investment resources. The production facilities were also being upgraded: the company acquired a new and much larger factory in the Bunbeg industrial estate. McDonnell always believed that new product development was the key to future growth.

By using distributors to develop export markets, he could focus his limited resources on developing better products.

The 'Gymbody 8'
In late 1993 the 'Gymbody 8' was launched, the first 'new' product to be produced by BioMedical Research Ltd. Designed primarily to meet the demands of a distributor in France, this *'Eight-pad stomach and bottom styler'* was soon to outsell all the company's other products combined. Although it was a much more stylish and portable product than anything else on the market at that time, initial sales of the Gymbody 8 were disappointing. Sales in general for home-use products were very limited. Most sales of home-use EMS-based consumer products were through mail order catalogues, small advertisements in the print media and a very limited number of retail outlets, mainly pharmacies. After a few months of lack-lustre sales performance, the French distributor tried using an American-style direct-response 'infomercial' on the national home-shopping channel, M6. This 30 minute 'chat-show', featuring interviews with a mixture of 'ordinary' and celebrity users of the Gymbody 8, produced immediate results. In between interviews and demonstrations showing how the product worked, viewers were encouraged to order a Gymbody 8 by phone. By the end of 1994 Gymbody 8 sales (ex-factory) to the French distributor were £3.4 million. The French promotional strategy also involved wide use of Direct Response (DR) advertisements in magazines and other print media. Over time retail distribution was extended to some pharmacies and a few sports stores. The soaring sales in France indicated a large untapped market for home-use EMS products, a market greater than anyone in the company had previously anticipated.

Other Slendertone markets were slower to grow - even after the introduction of the Gymbody 8. These markets included mainland Europe, South America, Japan and Australia. Sales in Ireland for the Gymbody 8 began to rise, but were small relative to the sales in France. The Gymbody 8 was listed in a few English mail-order catalogues, but sales were low. A distributor in Colombia was the only other customer of any significance for the Gymbody 8.

Distribution

With the exception of the home market, all sales of Slendertone were through distributors. By using distributors the company believed they could develop new markets for Slendertone (or re-develop previous markets) more cost-effectively and quickly. The company's marketing resources were very limited, given the investments being made in research and production. Some of the distributors had handled Slendertone products previously for BMR, while others were newly recruited. Most distributors tended to be small operators, sometimes working from their homes. Most did not have the resources to invest in large-scale market development. Efforts to attract larger distributors already in the beauty market were proving unsuccessful, in spite of the potential returns indicated by the ever-growing French market. Yet management were of the view that small distributors could also generate sales quickly using 'Direct Marketing'. Without the need to secure retail distribution, and with an immediate return on all promotional spend, going 'direct' would not require the levels of investment usually associated with introducing a new product to the market. The growing sales of Slendertone in Ireland from a range of direct marketing activities was proof of this.

Along with poorly-resourced and inexperienced distributors, sluggish growth in most markets was blamed on legal restrictions on Direct Response (DR) activity and cultural factors. In Germany, DR TV was not allowed[3]. Combined with a very low use of credit cards, this did not augur well for a DR-oriented strategy in Germany. Other countries also had restrictions on DR activities. With regard to cultural factors, a number of BioMedical Research personnel felt that the Germans were less likely to be interested in a product like Slendertone than the Spanish, the French or the South Americans. It was believed these latter countries had a stronger 'body culture' and their people were not as conservative as those in places like Germany or Switzerland . Yet, it was argued, this couldn't account for the rapidly growing sales of Slendertone in Ireland, a relatively conservative country.

---

3 Restrictions on DR activity in Germany, including TV broadcasts, have since been relaxed.

Direct Response Television

In the summer of 1995 a small cable TV company in Ireland agreed to broadcast a locally-produced infomercial. This infomercial featured local celebrities and studio guests, and adopted the French 'chat-show' format. Broadcast periodically throughout the summer to a potential audience of less than 200,000 viewers, this infomercial resulted in direct sales of almost one thousand Gymbody 8s. Sales of Gymbody 8s also increased in a handful of retail outlets located within the cable company's broadcast area. There also appeared to be an increase in demand for Slendertone beauty-salon treatments in this area. The success of the Irish infomercial campaign, along with the French campaign, convinced management that DR TV was the best way to sell Slendertone. It was believed that if infomercials worked well in both France and Ireland, it was likely they would work in most other countries. The focus of the sales strategy switched from developing local distributors to securing more DR TV opportunities. Intensive research was undertaken to identify infomercial opportunities across the globe: from South America to the Far East. A number of opportunities were identified, but the initial costs of producing infomercials for separate far-flung markets were a constraint. It was then decided to target 'home-shopping' companies. These companies buy TV time in many countries, and then broadcast a range of direct response programming.

By the end of 1995 a deal had been signed with Direct Shop Ltd., who were broadcasting home-shopping programming in over 30 countries at the time. The advantages of using Direct Shop were: that they had access to TV space across a number of markets; that they would handle all negotiations with the TV companies; that they would buy product up-front; and that they could handle large numbers of multi-lingual sales calls. BioMedical Research produced a new Slendertone infomercial exclusively for Direct Shop, using the successful 'chat show' format. Direct Shop ran the infomercial on satellite channels like Eurosport and Superchannel, usually late at night or early in the morning - when broadcasting time was available. The Slendertone infomercials were often broadcast alongside presentations for car care products, kitchen 'gadgets', fitness products / 'exercisers' and various other products. Direct Shop, like all TV home-shopping companies, operate on high margins. This meant that BioMedical Research would get less than 25% of the £120 retail price for the Gymbody 8. The company was selling this product to other distributors for around £40. Direct Shop also had a liberal 'customer returns' policy. This resulted in return rates of product from customers as high as 35%. Very often the outer packaging hadn't even been opened by the purchasers. Direct Shop also returned much unsold product, when TV sales were lower than expected for some countries.

Sales to Direct Shop were not as high initially as management had expected. After a few months sales began to increase, reaching monthly sales of around 3,000 Gymbody 8s. The majority of these sales were to TV viewers living in England.

The 'Direct Model'

Total sales of Slendertone continued to grow rapidly. Sales (ex-factory) to the French distributor were £5.6 million in 1995. By early 1996 it was looking like annual sales to France for that year would be considerably higher than the budgeted £7.2m. Irish sales for 1995 were £0.4m. and were well ahead of budget in early 1996. Sales to Direct Shop were on the increase, though not by as much as management had budgeted. Sales in the order of £0.75m were being made annually to the Colombian distributor. In early 1996 these four markets were accounting for over 90% of total Slendertone sales. Management continued to refine the 'direct model', given its success in these diverse markets.

One of the critical success factors of the direct approach was believed to be the way it allowed company representatives (either on the telephone directly to customers, or by extended TV appearances) to clearly explain how the product worked. Management felt it would not be so easy to sell this product through regular retail channels. Retail sales, it was thought, required too much explanation by sales staff, who themselves might not be very knowledgeable about the products. Retail was usually limited to pharmacies and some sports stores. There was no definite strategy for developing retail channels. It was thought that there were some people who did not want to buy 'direct', but who got their initial information from the infomercials, the company's telemarketing personnel, or other customers.

Going direct also allowed for more targeted marketing efforts. While the target market for Slendertone was defined as 'women between the ages of 25 and 55', a few niche segments were also targeted. These included 'pre-nuptials' , 'post-natals' and men. The post-natals were defined as women who had recently given birth and were now keen to regain their pre-pregnancy shape. Customer feedback had indicated that EMS was particularly effective in re-toning the stomach muscles which are normally 'stretched' during pregnancy. This segment was reached by means of direct response advertisements in magazines aimed at new mothers, and also the 'bounty bags' which are distributed in maternity wards. Bounty bags consist of free samples from manufacturers of baby-related products. The company would include a mone- off voucher along with a specially designed brochure explaining how the EMS can quickly and easily re-tone the stomach muscles. The pre-nuptials, those about to get married, were reached through wedding fairs and bridal magazines. EMS would allow the bride-to-be to quickly and easily tone up for the big day. It was also reported that increasing numbers of men were using the home-use products. As an optional accessory the company supplied non-stick rubber pads, which are attached to the body with a strap. These are suitable for men, for whom body-hair can make the adhesive pads uncomfortable.

Direct Response enabled the company to directly gauge the effectiveness of all advertising and promotions. Advertisements were placed in a range of media, using different copy, graphics and selling points, to identify the most effective advertising methods. Direct response also meant that every advertisement produced immediate revenue (or could be pulled quickly if it wasn't generating enough sales). This approach did not require the level of investment in brand development normally associated with introducing a new product to the market. In effect, all advertising became immediately self-financing.

Another important element of the 'direct' strategy was to allow the company to develop an extensive customer database, to be used to market other products that the company would develop in the future. It had not yet been decided what these products would be, other than that they would be sold under the 'Slendertone' brand. The database could also be used to sell other products of interest to Slendertone customers, and it could be traded with other companies. The personal data from customers also proved useful for research purposes, helping the company to identify its market.

Finally, for some customers, buying direct provided privacy when purchasing what some considered to be a 'personal' product. One Irish pharmacist, with a number of retail outlets, reported that some customers would buy a Slendertone product at a pharmacy far from where they lived - presumably to avoid recognition by staff or other customers. Some users of Slendertone products were reluctant to tell others they were using the company's products, even when complimented on how well they were looking. Reasons given included: "No one says they are using these gimmicks" and "because people would say to you, 'You don't need that'." Some customers were reluctant to tell even a spouse that they had bought, or were using, Slendertone.

Customer Feedback

These attitudes regarding the sensitive nature of the purchase were revealed in a focus group of Irish customers conducted in 1995. A number of favourable comments about the Gymbody 8 were recorded, such as, "It's fabulous, I lost inches around the waist, and my sister got it and she looks fantastic." Some of the comments reflected an initial doubt about the efficacy of the product, but subsequent satisfaction: "It's fabulous, I'm delighted, it's wonderful - it does actually work." One user was not so satisfied: "It's not very effective, I didn't see a visible difference, no one else did - no one commented."

The majority of the participants thought it represented very good value at £99. In determining 'value' they tended to compare it to the cost of: EMS treatment in a salon; joining a gym; taking fitness classes; or exercise equipment. The research also revealed generally low long-term usage of the product. One issue raised related to uncertainty about using the unit, particularly on how to place the pads on the body correctly. Another issue that arose was that using the products involved a certain amount of 'hassle': attaching the pads to the unit, placing the pads on the body, actually using it for 40 minutes and then putting it all away again. All the focus group participants had bought their unit 'off the TV', having seen the Irish infomercial. Most thought the infomercial was very effective in explaining the product, and that "it looked like a good product." Some found the TV presentation to be interesting, and even entertaining (with people watching it a number of times), while others thought it was "a bit over the top" or "false-looking."

The findings of this research supported anecdotal evidence and customer service feedback being received by company personnel: initial doubt about the product's efficacy, a certain amount of surprise that it actually worked, mixed satisfaction (though mostly very high) with the results attained, and low long-term usage. The low usage levels were confirmed by the low levels of replacement sales of the adhesive pads (these are used with the home-use units to apply the current to the body, and need to be replaced after 35 / 40 uses).

The Competition
Slendertone was the only product of its kind being marketed on TV in 1995. A number of new EMS products entered the market during the mid 1990s, using a similar 'direct response' approach in magazines, mail order catalogues and other media. Other products had been available for many years previously, sold mostly through the mail-order channel. With the exception of 'Ultratone', an English product, the competitor products in almost all markets tended to be of much poorer quality than Slendertone (though they were not necessarily much cheaper to buy). In this very fragmented market there were no international leaders. For instance, in Italy, there were at least eight products on the market, none of which was being sold outside the country. Other than the occasional mail-order product, there did not appear to be any EMS units for sale in Germany. Ultratone was one of the biggest players in England but did not sell in France, then estimated to be the largest market for EMS products. In Spain a poor-quality product called the 'Gymshape 8' was launched; it was priced lower than the 'Gymbody 8.'

Management saw Slendertone as being at the 'top-end' of the market, based on its superior quality. Although the company had by now lost most of its mail-order business to lower priced (and lower quality) competitors, management's attitude was that the biggest and most lucrative markets still lay untapped. It was felt the company had the products and the 'know-how' to exploit these markets, as evidenced in France and Ireland. However, the increasing competition continued to put pressure on prices; most of the cost-savings being achieved through more efficient production were being passed on to the distributors. From 1993 to the beginning of 1996 the retail price of the 'Gymbody 8' had fallen over £40 in France. In order to satisfy the French distributor's demand for cheaper products for certain channels, a 'low price' range, under the 'Minibody' and 'Intone' brands, was launched by BioMedical Research. These products did not feature the Slendertone logo anywhere.

Given the fragmented nature of the market, and a complete lack of secondary data for the EMS product class, it was hard to establish what market share different companies had. Lack of data also made it difficult to determine the size of the existing market for EMS products in each country. For planning purposes the company focused on the potential market for EMS, based on the belief that most countries had a large latent demand for EMS-based cosmetic products. Potential demand for each country was calculated on the basis of the sizes of the target market and the niche segments in that country. As revealed in the market research findings, the competition also had to be viewed in terms of the other means to improve body shape: the gym, fitness classes, exercise equipment, diets, diet-foods etc.

The Professional Market
The salon business in Ireland experienced a big revival during the mid-1990s. The extensive marketing for the home-use products helped to create new, or renewed, awareness among salon users of EMS treatments, and the Slendertone brand. Intensive media campaigns in Ireland were run to promote the salon products. In conjunction with salons, the company placed full page 'feature' advertisements in papers like the Sunday Independent. A certain amount of tension arose between the company and the salon owners, due to the company simultaneously marketing salon and home-use units. For the price of 15 salon treatments one could buy a 'Gymbody 8.'

The re-development of the salon market during the mid-1990s attracted a number of competitors to Ireland. These included Ultratone, Eurowave, CACI and Arysis. The increased competition led to greater promotional activity, which in turn increased the demand for salon EMS treatments. Even though Slendertone had become a generic term for salon EMS treatment in Ireland, research in early 1996 indicated that some customers thought it represented 'old' technology. Ultratone had been positioning itself as the product with 'newer' technology, one which was more effective, more comfortable and offered faster results - in spite of using very similar, if not more basic, technology. BioMedical Research was promoting the fact, in 1996, that Slendertone had been in existence for 30 years. A special 30th anniversary logo featured on the promotional literature for the professional market. This was done to give buyers the assurance of long-term company marketing support and technical back-up in the face of many new entrants into the market. There was little effort being made by the international distributors to develop the professional market in other countries, in spite of very high margins on the larger professional units (which retailed at over £4,000). The French distributor was showing no interest in the professional market in France. They believed the size of the home-use market offered much greater potential - and it did not require a sales team.

Product Development

After the success of the Gymbody 8, a number of other home-use EMS products were developed by BioMedical Research before 1996. These were primarily designed to meet the requirements of the French distributor. Along with the low-cost Minibody and InTone brands, products developed under the Slendertone brand included the 'Bustyler' (for lifting the breasts), the 'Face Up' (a facial anti-ageing unit) and the 'Celluforme' (to combat cellulite). Little market research was undertaken by the company when developing these products. (The research that was done mostly consisted of prototype testing on a number of volunteers recruited locally in Galway, Ireland). The products would be developed, mostly in-house, according to criteria determined by the French distributor. The distributor also indicated the cost at which units would have to be supplied to them, so that they could achieve certain retail price points in the channels which they were targeting.

Rapid Growth

In March 1996 it was looking as if annual Slendertone sales (ex-factory) could break the £10 million barrier by year-end. Sales for the Gymbody 8 represented over 70% of all Slendertone sales (including professional units). Over 75% of Gymbody 8 units being produced were for the French distributor. New employees were being recruited in a number of areas, including a large number of temporary workers in production. Many other workers chose to work overtime. There was a real sense of excitement throughout the company as orders continued to increase. The potential for Slendertone was enormous. If other countries achieved even a quarter of the per capita sales levels being attained in France or Ireland, the company would soon be a major Irish exporter. Plans were being drawn up to extend the factory and to build a new headquarters in Galway. In spite of the impressive growth, and the exciting potential, the board of the company was very concerned about the growing dependence on one distributor.

The French distributor was becoming more and more demanding with regard to margins, product development and pricing strategies. They continued to develop their own promotional material for the Slendertone range. The products were being sold as a form of 'effortless exercise': "the equivalent of 240 sit-ups in just 40 minutes, while watching TV!." Some advertising featured topless models alongside sensational claims for the products' effectiveness - "the body you've always wanted in just three weeks." The distributor in France had arranged in 1996 for a well-known blonde TV celebrity to endorse the product. In the words of one of the Irish marketing staff, the distributor's approach was "very tacky" (see exhibit A). Still, few could argue with the ever-increasing sales. The distributor appeared to have found a large market that responded favourably to this type of promotion. Analysis of the French sales database, which was not computerised, indicated that sales were mostly to younger C1C2 females. However, the distributor was very reluctant to share sales data with the company.

Developing the UK Market

A number of marketing meetings were held in April 1996 to develop a plan to reduce the company's growing dependence on this one customer. It was decided to develop the UK market directly, without any distributor involvement. This decision was made on the basis of a number of factors: the failure to attract good distributors in the past, the success of the company's own direct campaign in Ireland, the reasonably successful sales to UK viewers by Direct Shop and, finally, geographical and cultural proximity to Ireland.

In May 1996 the board supported management's decision to develop the English market directly. This was going to require a substantial investment, both in terms of money and management time. By the end of July an office had been established in London, with a general manager and two staff. Direct response advertisements were soon being placed in a number of different print media, from The Sunday Times Magazine to the News of the World's colour supplement. Responses and sales were closely monitored to gauge the more likely market for the products. Sales were slow to grow; by the end of the first quarter the UK subsidiary was behind budget. The cost of maintaining an office in London was also impacting on company profitability. However, the Slendertone staff in both Ireland and England were optimistic about the longer-term prospects.

SLENDERTONE - PART TWO

Slendertone in Turmoil

In late 1996 the size of the orders from the French distributor started to fall. Uncertainty about the reason for the sudden fall in French sales abounded, particularly as it was the build-up to the normally busy Christmas market. The company quickly went from having a healthy cash surplus to being overdrawn. The banks were putting pressure on the company to address the situation. A decision was made to lay off all the temporary production workers. The situation continued to deteriorate. Over £1.5m of raw material and stock, mostly for the French market, had now accumulated in the factory. Staff were wondering whether the company could survive. McDonnell and his management team persevered with the plan to develop the UK market, while addressing the serious situation developing in France.

After the slow start, sales in the UK were now starting to grow. Most sales were coming from direct response advertisements in magazines. Much public relations activity was also being undertaken. Limited distribution had been secured in some nation-wide retail chains, mostly on a trial basis in a few stores. Sales to Direct Shop (the TV home-shopping company) were still disappointing, never rising above 4,000 Gymbody 8s a month. Sales in Ireland were up over 30% on the previous year. Though sales to Ireland were now the highest, per capita, of any market, they were still less than 10% of total sales. Sales to Colombia were about the same, while all the other distributors were down a little on the previous year.

The market in France deteriorated rapidly in early 1997. Subsequent analysis indicated a number of factors contributing to the dramatic loss of business in France. The distributor had lost the TV slot for the Gymbody 8 to a cheaper product. Other Direct Response channels seemed to have become 'exhausted', or were being filled by cheaper products. To compound matters, a feature on EMS products in a consumer magazine gave poor ratings to many of the home-use products in the market. Although the Slendertone product range received the highest rating, this did not protect the company. A number of the low-quality competitors suddenly pulled out of the market, leaving a bad feeling in the trade. The trade consisted of

Direct Marketing companies who bought product from the distributors or manufacturers to sell to their existing customer base. It also included retailers - mostly pharmacies, sports shops and a few department stores. The sudden fall in advertising for EMS products affected market demand, and left many traders with unsold product. By the time BioMedical Research had received this information it was too late to take any action. The company terminated its relationship with the French distributor later in the year, and all Slendertone sales in France soon came to an end.

At about the same time management ended their relationship with Direct Shop. The combination of lower-than-expected sales, low margins and high return rates ensured that it was never going to be a profitable undertaking for the company. Furthermore, some tension with existing distributors arose when Direct Shop began to broadcast across Europe, in many cases offering a price for the Gymbody 8 that was lower than what the distributors were charging for it locally. At least the company's own sales to the UK were growing. By selling direct to customers in the UK BioMedical Research was earning a healthy margin (though the cost of the UK office and the increasing number of promotional campaigns had to be covered).

Restructuring
There had been a widespread belief throughout the company for many years that, in the words of one manager, "more marketing was needed." Efforts in 1995 and early 1996 to recruit a 'marketing manager / marketing director designate', using advertisements in the Irish and UK recruitment pages, were unsuccessful. It was suggested that the credibility issue concerning Slendertone might also be having an effect on recruitment. With added urgency, the company succeeded in attracting O'Donohoe to the job of marketing director for Slendertone in April 1997. O'Donohoe had gained extensive marketing experience with Waterford Glass. He saw the opportunity to develop the Slendertone brand, and welcomed the responsibility the job offered, but he admits it wasn't easy at first: "When I joined in April I had to go out to France and everyone here in the office and factory would be waiting when I came back to see

if I had got any new orders." Recognising the opportunity being presented by the trial placements for the Gymbody 8 in various UK stores, he immediately focused on developing the company's relationships in the retail channel.

While working on increasing retail sales, O'Donohoe also initiated extensive research into the various markets for Slendertone. He started to build up a clearer picture of the markets for Slendertone, and its brand positioning. His analysis of the French market identified the reasons for the drop in sales. It also revealed that Slendertone was not, nor had it ever been, the market leader in France. Based on the distributor's reports, the company had been under the impression that Slendertone had some 70% of the home-use EMS market. O'Donohoe's findings revealed that Slendertone market share was only a fraction of this figure. His analysis also revealed that sales of replacement pads had always been extremely low, indicating low customer product-usage; it had previously been presumed that the French distributor was using a different supplier for the replacement pads. Focus group research in a number of countries showed that Slendertone had a very confused positioning: it was variously associated with dieting, weight-loss, health, fitness, exercise, toning and body-shaping. The focus groups also reinforced the credibility issue. Many people's first thought on seeing the product being advertised was "Does it work?" Secondary data showed the size of the different markets for areas such as health, fitness, cosmetics etc. in different countries. O'Donohoe also gathered data on consumer behaviour and motivations relating to these different markets.

The Business Defined

The next stage for O'Donohoe was to decide exactly what business the company was in. "I've read about this business being described as everything from the 'EMS business', whatever that is, to 'passive gymnastics'! Our consumer research showed that Slendertone had a very confused message. We're in the self-confidence business," he states emphatically, "self confidence through improved appearance." He now defines the Slendertone brand as: 'the most effective and convenient appearance solutions.' The new slogan for Slendertone will be:

'living life and loving it.' In terms of people's deeper motivations with regard to health and fitness activities, O'Donohoe
stresses a core need to look good. He states that most people
are working out to look good rather than to be healthy.
Likewise, "people will diet, not for the sake of losing weight,
but to improve their appearance through their weight-loss." It
is this core need of looking good which O'Donohoe is targeting
with Slendertone. In spite of the company's involvement in the
health market (with its NeuroTech range of products),
O'Donohoe is clear that Slendertone is about appearance and
not health. He sees it as misleading to talk in terms of 'health
and beauty,' a trade category into which many products are
placed. He puts a value of $170bn on the 'self-confidence' mar-
ket in Europe.[4] This figure includes the combined markets for
cosmetics and fashion.

Also included in this market are men. Originally only recognised as a niche segment, male users now represent an important and fast-growing market for EMS cosmetic products. In
late 1997 BioMedical Research modified the Gymbody 8
(adding rubber pads and re-designing the packaging) and
launched the 'Gymbody for Men'. This was very successful and
opened up a new market segment for Slendertone.

The company has begun extensive consumer trials at a clin-
ic in Galway to gain a better understanding of the exact phys-
iological benefits of Slendertone - and particularly to identify
new ways of measuring these benefits. According to O'Donohoe,
"we want to get away from the earlier measurements of effectiveness, such as 'inch loss'". He is conscious of the added psychological benefits that these products might offer users.
BioMedical's researchers are also using these trials to identify
ways to improve product convenience and comfort.

Re-positioning *Slendertone*
By early 1999, Slendertone products were being stocked in over
2,300 retail outlets, primarily in the UK. O'Donohoe states that
the increasing emphasis on retail has to be seen in terms of a
complete re-positioning of the Slendertone brand. "Using

---

4 The FDA restricts the use of EMS for cosmetic purposes in the USA - see
   Appendix

Direct Shop [TV home-shopping] was the worst thing ever for this company. And look at these [French] magazine advertisements: lots of exclamation marks, sensational product claims, very cluttered, and the models used!", he remarks, reviewing the earlier marketing of Slendertone. O'Donohoe says it is these promotional tactics which have resulted in a 'gadget' positioning for Slendertone - one he is now working on changing. Furthermore, he says, by making excessive product claims the company was unlikely to meet customer expectations. This was jeopardising the opportunity for repeat purchases of Slendertone products by existing customers. Gone, says O'Donohoe, are the promises of 'effortless exercise'; "we are telling customers they need to work with the products to get results. This is resulting in a different type of customer for Slendertone - we want to get away from the gadget-freaks." It is this different type of customer that O'Donohoe hopes will also purchase other Slendertone-branded products in the future. The target market for Slendertone now is women and men aged 20 to 60 years old. The earlier niche segments, like the post-natals, are no longer being targeted separately. O'Donohoe believes it is important to keep the Slendertone message focused, rather than having different messages for different segments of the market.

Central to O'Donohoe's strategy is the development of Slendertone into a brand in its own right. From now on O'Donohoe wants people to associate Slendertone with 'effective and convenient appearance solutions' rather than EMS devices; "Slendertone will be a brand that just happens to have EMS products." The Slendertone range could, in the future, include many types of products. The company has just created a new position, that of Brand Extensions Manager, to plan the development of the Slendertone range. O'Donohoe believes the company is now in a position to create an international brand. "People will tell you it takes hundreds of millions to create an international brand - we don't agree."

A priority for O'Donohoe, in his goal to develop the Slendertone brand, is an increased emphasis on the 'Slendertone' name. As well as a re-design of all the product packaging, to reflect more 'real' users in 'real' situations (see exhibits B and C), all the product names have been changed.

The original 'Gymbody 8' will now be marketed as the 'Slendertone Body'. The 'Face Up' is now the 'Slendertone Face' and the 'Celluforme' becomes the 'Slendertone Body Plus'. The male products will be the 'Slendertone Body Profile' and the 'Slendertone Body Profile Sports', which has been adapted from the 'Total Body' unit. Along with the 'Slendertone Total Body', these products constitute the full Slendertone home-use range, reduced from some 25 products three years previously. A new professional unit, utilising innovative touch-screen technology and 'space-age' design, is also about to be launched. O'Donohoe sees the professional market playing an important role in the development of Slendertone. He does not believe that the home-use and professional markets are competing - the company's experience has been that promotions for the home-use products raise awareness (and custom) for the professional market. The company currently has four staff dedicated to developing the professional market in the UK.

Accessing the Market

O'Donohoe continues to put greater emphasis on developing retail channels, which he says, "still represent over 95% of sales for all products sold world-wide, in spite of the current hype about direct marketing." He believes he is able to secure retail space from important multiples because he is offering them unique access to the body-shape section of the appearance market. For these retailers Slendertone represents a new category of good, with higher than average revenues. On a shop-shelf 'mock-up', in a small room at the back of the office, there is a display of the new Slendertone range, alongside massagers and shavers and other personal care products. O'Donohoe is conscious of the attention Slendertone has been attracting from the big players in the personal care market. In some cases they have been losing vital shelf space to this relatively unknown company from Ireland. He believes BioMedical Research's expertise in the marketing of EMS products, a strong brand and greater company flexibility (due to its smaller size), will enable the company to defend itself from the multi-national companies now looking at the EMS market.

The focus on retail does not mean an end to the use of direct marketing. Direct sales still account for around half of all UK sales. O'Donohoe sees direct marketing continuing to play an important role in developing the UK and newer markets. The new direct response advertisements have been changed to reflect the move towards a stronger Slendertone brand identity, and away from the 'oversell' of earlier years (see exhibit D).

The company will continue to use distributors for some markets. However, O'Donohoe is determined to have greater company control over the brand than in the past. By maintaining "control of the message" he believes the company can avoid a recurrence of what happened in the French market. Through a strong brand identity and a carefully controlled and differentiated image, he intends to protect the Slendertone name and market from the activities of other EMS companies. He does not plan to compete on price with the lower quality producers; he believes that by investing in the Slendertone brand the company will be able to offer the customer greater total value at a higher price. The company will develop important markets like Germany and France directly, as they have done successfully in the UK. Slendertone offices in Frankfurt and Paris have just been opened. O'Donohoe is conscious of the cost of establishing and maintaining international operations and the need to develop these markets successfully and promptly.

Slendertone: **The Future**
The company views the potential for Slendertone on two fronts: the existing potential for EMS-based products (including the existing Slendertone range and new improved EMS products) and the potential for non-EMS Slendertone products. O'Donohoe believes he can restore Slendertone's fortunes in the French market: "the need is still there". He is conscious of bad feeling which may still exist within the trade, but other companies are operating again in this market (including BioMedical's former distributor, who now sells a lower quality EMS product). There is still a lack of published secondary data for the EMS cosmetic market in any country. It is believed that the UK is now the largest EMS market, by a significant degree. Company research indicates that the other markets with any significant EMS sales are Spain and Italy. There is currently little EMS sales activity being observed by the company in Germany. Working off the level of sales now being attained in

Ireland (which have continued to grow every year since 1991) and the phenomenal recent growth in England, combined with a universal desire to look good, O'Donohoe envisages rapid growth for the existing Slendertone range in the short-term. The potential for the extended Slendertone range in the longer-term is much greater. Realising this potential will depend on how effective the marketing strategy is in addressing all the issues, and how well it is implemented.

For some the question might remain: can Kevin McDonnell succeed in offering self-confidence to millions around the world from a factory in the wilds of Donegal? Certainly the locals in Bunbeg wouldn't doubt it.

EXHIBIT A: A COPY OF DIRECT RESPONSE
ADVERTISEMENT USED IN FRANCE

EXHIBIT B: THE COVER OF THE 'GYMBODY 8' CASE (USED SINCE 1994)

EXHIBIT C: THE COVER OF THE 'SLENDERTONE BODY' CASE (INTRODUCED IN 1999)

EXHIBIT D: THE NEW ADVERTISEMENT FOR THE 'SLENDERTONE BODY'

APPENDIX: WHAT IS SLENDERTONE?

Beauty salons buy Electronic Muscle Stimulation (EMS) units, such as *Slendertone*, so they can provide their customers with a toning/body-shaping treatment. EMS devices work by delivering a series of electric charges to the muscle, via pads placed on the skin over the muscle area. Each tiny electric charge 'fires' the motor-points in the muscle. These are similar to the natural charges sent by the brain, through the nervous system, to activate particular muscles and thus cause movement. EMS therefore has the effect of exercising the muscle, but without any need to move the rest of the body. Customers use the EMS treatment over a period of weeks to help tone a particular area, primarily with the aim of improving body shape. Treatment can also improve circulation and the texture of the skin. EMS gives users improved body-shape through improved muscle tone, rather than through weight loss. Customers typically book a series of 10 or 15 one-hour treatments, to be administered once or twice weekly. A qualified beautician, trained in the use of EMS (as part of the standard professional training for beauticians), administers the treatment in the salon. A series of ten salon treatments in Ireland costs in the range of £70. An alternative salon treatment to tone muscles is a manual 'toning table' which works the muscles by moving various parts of the body attached to the table. Home-use EMS units allow users to treat themselves in the comfort, privacy and convenience of their own home. A home-use unit like the *Slendertone Body* currently retails for £100 in Ireland. In terms of treatment, the home-use unit should offer the user similar results to a salon treatment, if used correctly and consistently.

Some customers prefer to go to a salon for EMS treatment, possibly enjoying the professional attention they get in a salon environment, and the break it offers from everyday life. Booking and paying for a series of treatments in a salon also encourages customers to complete the treatment. Others prefer the convenience, privacy and economy offered by the home-use units. However, the home treatment requires a certain discipline to use the unit regularly. Home-users sometimes report that they are uncertain if they are using their unit correctly. This is mostly to do with proper pad placement. EMS has been available in salons for over 30 years, but the home-use market only began to develop significantly in the last 10 years.

Is EMS / Slendertone Safe?

EMS was originally developed for medical use. A common application of EMS includes rehabilitation of a muscle after an accident, or a stroke. EMS is also frequently used by physio-therapists for muscle rehabilitation after sports and other injuries. *Slendertone* was developed to enable healthy users to 'exercise' muscles without having to do any exercise. By remaining seated, lying down, or even doing minor chores, users could get the benefit of a vigorous work-out. The effect of EMS is similar to that of regular exercise on a muscle. For many years the company compared the effect of using EMS (as applied to the abdominal muscles) to the effect gained from doing sit-ups. With the exception of well-stated contra-indica-tions (EMS should not be used by pregnant women, on or near open wounds, on or near ulcers, by diabetics, on or near the throat area) EMS has been proven to be perfectly safe for a variety of uses. Some people wonder what might happen when you stop using EMS. Again, the effect is like taking regular exercise: if you stop you may regain the shape you had before you started exercising.

The FDA (Food and Drug Administration in the USA) have classified this type of EMS-based product as a 'Class II' device. Class II devices must be prescribed by a 'licensed practitioner' and only for very specified medical purposes. The FDA regula-tions governing the sale and use of EMS devices are based on proven efficacy and safety. According to the FDA there is insuf-ficient clinical evidence to support claims such as 'body-shap-ing', 'weight-loss' or 'cellulite removal' for EMS treatments. The FDA's decision to impose stringent controls on the use of EMS was made after a number of home-use EMS users suffered minor injuries. Users of a direct-current, home-use EMS unit available in the USA in the 1970s suffered skin 'burns' around the pad placement area. All *Slendertone* products, like the other cosmetic EMS products on the market today, only use alternating current, which will not cause burns.

STRATEGIC MARKETING FOR EDUCATION IN A DIVIDED SOCIETY

John Milliken and Tony Gallagher

INTRODUCTION

It has been suggested that the problems of segregated education, conflict and the division of societies are at least as old as the history of formal education in Ireland. Since 1969, Northern Ireland has suffered the longest period of civil disorder and unrest in its history and, despite numerous efforts over recent years, the conflict remains unresolved. While the conflict is not simply about religion, the primary social division within Northern Ireland lies between the Protestant and Catholic communities. A particular feature of the education system in Northern Ireland is the existence of parallel school systems for Protestants and Catholics. Not surprisingly, right from the outbreak of political violence there were numerous calls for change in the educational system to encourage Catholic and Protestant children to attend the same schools.

Against the backdrop of the long-standing, violent conflict in Northern Ireland a number of parents believed that if children went to school together some of the mutual ignorance about each other's culture might be reduced. In 1974, ACT - All Children Together - was established by a group of parents and others to try to persuade existing schools to change to integrated schools. As part of their efforts a bill was passed through parliament by Lord Dunleath, which would allow existing schools to make such a change in status. The parents from different parts of the community approached the existing non-denominational schools, controlled by the Northern Ireland Education and Library Boards. These schools were asked to consider changing their structures and ethos to become more welcoming to parents of all religions. However, despite the apparent popular support for integrated schools, and the legal facility for change, no school actually changed status. Frustrated by the lack of response, the parents themselves decided to open a 'model' integrated school to prove the viability of their approach. Thus, in 1981, they set up a second-level school which became Lagan College, the first planned integrated post-primary school in Northern Ireland.

Three years later a second pressure group, BELTIE - the Belfast Trust for Integrated Education -was formed. The combined efforts of these two groups resulted in the development of three new integrated schools in 1985. Without government assistance, these schools had to be independently financed. In 1986 The Department of Education for Northern Ireland (DENI) agreed to provide grant aid to Lagan College. By 1988, eight integrated schools, all funded by parents, had been established. Some ten year later the number of schools has risen to forty-two, and includes nursery, primary and second level colleges.

EDUCATIONAL MARKETS

The Education Reform Act (1988), and its implementation in Northern Ireland under the Education Reform Order (1989), was designed to establish a market in education. Society has also changed in its structure, norms, aspirations, behaviour and values. As a result of economic and income growth, demands have moved beyond basic survival needs to the fulfilment of psychological aspirations. The balance of population numbers has changed and the resultant outcome has been an altered perspective in culture. These changing expectations of the consumer have far-reaching implications for schools which have necessitated schools becoming more responsive to their external environment.

The initial change has been the developing relationship between schools and their communities whereby schools now view themselves as an integral part of their community. The second change has been evidenced in the schools' relationships with local authorities (Education and Library Boards in Northern Ireland) where the schools are now being actively encouraged to manage their own external relations. The changing culture of today's pupils and students is the third factor and it has significant implications for appropriate teaching and learning styles and a consequential impact on resources.

These multifarious cultural factors are made even more complex for integrated education in Northern Ireland by the stance of the churches on their role in education. In 1975, for example, Catholic Bishop Philbin said that: "There is no greater injury that can be done to Catholicism than interference with the character and identity of our schools" (Philbin 1975), and the Catholic

Church has remained lukewarm to the new sector ever since. Similarly, the Protestant churches have tended to be defensive about the existing state schools. In part, both sets of views are influenced by a perception that the development of new integrated schools inevitably leads to a zero-sum situation since surplus capacity already exists throughout the school system.

THE INTEGRATED ETHOS

The structure, staffing and enrolments in integrated schools are quite different from those in the traditional sectors. Religious and cultural diversity is both valued and celebrated and pupil enrolment is guided by the principle that no ethnic religious grouping should be dominant. The schools are supposed to be all ability at both primary and second-level and are stated to be, "child-centred in seeking to maximise the potential of all children in their educational and social development."

CO-ORDINATION AND DIRECTION

As this integrated movement gained momentum through the 1980s a central forum and umbrella organization was formed, in 1989, to act as a focal point and facilitator for the movement- the Northern Ireland Council for Integrated Education (NICIE) NICIE holds charitable status and obtains core funding from the Department of Education. According to NICIE (1995) its role is to:

> ... assist the development of planned integrated education and schools in Northern Ireland for the public benefit.

DEVELOPMENT AND GROWTH

The integrated situation developed further with the Education Reform Order (1989), the Northern Ireland equivalent of the Education Reform Act. While the Order contained many of the reforms initiated in England and Wales, it also contained some measures specifically designed to promote better community relations in Northern Ireland. These included a formal commitment, for the first time, by government to support the development of integrated schools, new curricular initiatives on community relations as part of the common curriculum, and support for contact programmes between existing Protestant and Catholic schools. In addition, the parents of pupils in an existing school could vote to change, or transform, its status to an integrated school.

Under this legislation, new integrated schools qualified for

Government grants immediately, even if they were small, so long as there were reasonable prospects for growth. Integrated schools became eligible for 100 per cent funding, though in the case of new schools, grants for capital development were still not available until viability had been established. In 1992, the Government was also co-founder, along with the Nuffield Trust and the Joseph Rowntree Foundation, of an independently administered capital fund for the promotion of integrated education. The government's policy on integrated education was reaffirmed by the Northern Ireland Secretary of State, Sir Patrick Mayhew, at the opening of Saints and Scholars Integrated Primary (Armagh) in June 1995 when he stated his wish to see integrated schools wherever there was sufficient parental demand. At present there are forty-four integrated schools, comprising a little under three per cent of the total pupil enrolment.

While those involved with the integrated schools movement clearly welcomed the new supportive policy environment, some have felt that the rhetoric has not been matched by practical concrete support. Thus, for example, NICIE's 1995 annual report complained that the development of integrated schools was being severely hampered by a lack of financial support. NICIE argued that existing integrated schools were obliged to operate from mobile classrooms and that, while six of the then existing integrated schools operated entirely from mobile classrooms, they were placed at the bottom of the DENI capital priority list. This situation was exacerbated, NICIE felt, by the suspension of permanent extensions in 1994. Furthermore, NICIE felt that DENI was not prepared to support new schools in some circumstances where parental support could be demonstrated. The problem, of course, is that opening new schools is a more expensive way to develop integrated schools as opposed to transforming existing ones. But, of the forty-four existing integrated schools, only twelve have resulted from transformations and six of those within the last year. In addition, while NICIE is likely to welcome more transformations, it is unclear what form the integrated nature of transformed schools would take. At its simplest we can describe it as follows: NICIE encourages new integrated schools to maintain a balance among pupils and staff such that the minority community will not fall below 40 per cent. If such a threshold was set in order to transform an existing school, however, very few would ever qualify. For this reason transformation can occur when the minority enrolment is as little as 10 per cent, albeit with the proviso that there should be a reasonable expectation that it will increase. However, since the whole process of transformation can, in any case, proceed without NICIE involvement, there is a risk that the integrated nature of new schools might become discredited and the standing of the whole sector be put at risk.

Demographic Trends

Since the turn of the century, the trends in the age structure in Northern Ireland have been quite significant with the number of 0-14 year olds reducing by approximately one-third and only accounting for 24% of the population as opposed to more than 30 per cent in 1971. There has also been a corresponding increase in the percentage representation by the older age groups which has implications for other public services.

TABLE 1 : TRENDS IN AGE STRUCTURE, NORTHERN IRELAND, 1901-1991

Age	0-14	15-44	45-64	65+
1901	31	47	17	5
1911	30	46	16	8
1921	29	45	19	7
1931	27	46	19	8
1951	28	42	20	10
1961	29	40	21	10
1971	31	39	19	11
1981	26	42	20	12
1991	24	44	19	13

Source: N.I.E.C. (Figures are expressed as a % of population)

The revised census estimates from 1991 suggest that more than 30 per cent of the Catholic population are under the age of 16 in comparison with those grouped as other denominations who account for just 22 per cent. The demand by the Catholic population for education is much greater than that of the Protestant community and is reflected in the government expenditure levels. However, approximately 7 out of every 10 individuals of retirement age are Protestant resulting in greater expenditure on services for the elderly.

TABLE 2 : DISTRIBUTION OF NI BIRTHS AND BIRTH
RATES BY DENOMINATION 1971-1987

Year	Total Number	% Catholic	Birth Rates/1000 Catholic	Birth Rates/1000 Other denominations
1971	31,765	45.0	25.5	18.5
1972	29,994	45.5	24.5	17.5
1973	29,200	46.0	24.0	17.0
1974	27,160	46.5	22.0	15.0
1975	26,130	46.5	22.0	15.0
1976	26,361	47.0	22.0	15.0
1977	25,437	48.5	21.0	14.0
1978	26,239	49.5	22.5	14.5
1979	28,178	49.5	23.5	15.0
1980	28,582	49.5	24.0	15.5
1981	27,302	50.0	23.0	14.5
1982	27,028	51.0	23.0	14.0
1983	27,255	50.0	22.0	14.5
1984	27,693	50.0	22.0	15.0
1985	27,635	49.5	22.0	15.0
1986	28,152	49.0	22.0	15.0
1987	27,865	48.5	21.5	15.5

Source: Annuario Pontifico

Recent Research

In 1996 a senior development officer with NICIE felt that, with
thirty-two schools then open, it was time to carry out some
research to determine the market position of the movement. It
was also believed that with the introduction of local management
of schools it would be important to determine the level of market
awareness of each school, how they viewed each other and how
they regarded the services of the umbrella organization NICIE.

A questionnaire was sent out to each school principal and, at
the same time, one was sent to the directors of NICIE as the policy makers of the integrated education movement. The response
rate was interesting in that 80% of the schools responded but only

30% of the directors of NICIE responded. The results are included in the following tables.

TABLE 3 : SCHOOLS IN SURVEY (n=32)

Population	Total	Responses	%
Primary Schools	21	17	81
Second Level Colleges	9	7	78
Total Schools	30	24	80
N.I.C.I.E. Directors *	12	4	33

*One of the directors is also a school principal and was included only in the schools' survey

TABLE 4 : PERCENTAGE OF PUPILS COMING FROM
AN INTEGRATED ESTABLISHMENT
(i.e. from Nursery to Primary and from Primary
to Second Level Colleges)

Value %	Frequency	Percent	Valid Percent	Cum. Percent
0	15	62.5	62.5	62.5
20	2	8.3	8.3	70.8
21	2	8.3	8.3	79.2
25	1	4.2	4.2	83.3
50	1	4.2	4.2	87.5
60	1	4.2	4.2	91.7
80	1	4.2	4.2	95.8
85	1	4.2	4.2	100.0
Total	24	100.0	100.0	

TABLE 5 : MARKETING ACTIVITIES (VALID CASES =24)

Category Label	Code	Count	% of Responses	% of Cases
Yes	1	2	4.4	8.3
No	2	4	8.9	16.7
Press	3	14	31.1	58.3
Open Day	4	8	17.8	33.3
Leaflets	5	7	15.6	29.2
Prospectus	6	2	4.4	8.3
TV/Radio	7	2	4.4	8.3
Fund-raising	8	1	2.2	4.2
Visit Schools	9	5	11.1	20.8
Total		*45	100.0	187.7

TABLE 6 : PERCEIVED CUSTOMERS OF INTEGRATED EDUCATION

Value	Frequency	Percent	Valid Percent	Cum. Percent
Children	1	4.2	4.2	4.2
Parents	3	12.5	12.5	16.7
DENI	1	4.2	4.2	20.8
Parents & children	10	41.7	41.7	62.5
Parents, children & DENI	2	8.3	8.3	70.8
Parents, children & staff	3	12.5	12.5	83.3
Parents, children, staff & DENI	1	4.2	4.2	87.5

TABLE 7 : PERCEIVED COMPETITORS OF INTEGRATED
EDUCATION

Category Label	Code	Count	% of Responses	% of Cases
Local schools	1	12	46.2	57.1
Controlled schools	2	6	23.1	28.6
Grammar schools	3	3	11.5	14.3
Maintained schools	4	3	11.5	14.3
Lack of space ****	5	1	3.8	4.8
Parents' attitudes	6	1	3.8	4.8
Totals		26	100.0	123.8

TABLE 8 : HOW WELL N.I.C.I.E. IS PERCEIVED AS
FULFILLING ITS ROLE(S)

Value Label	Value	Frequency	Percent	Valid Percent	Cum. Percent
Very well	1	4	16.7	16.6	16.6
Well	2	10	41.7	41.7	58.3
Average	3	8	33.3	33.3	91.6
Poor	4	1	4.2	4.2	95.8
Very poor	5	1	4.2	4.2	100.0
		24	100.0	100.0	

TABLE 9:1 : SOCIETAL IMPACTS ON INTEGRATED EDUCATION (7 MISSING CASES - 17 VALID CASES)

Category Label	Code	Count	% of Responses	% of Cases
Population Change	1	11	55.0	64.7
Transport	2	3	15.0	17.6
Staff Bias	3	1	5.0	5.9
Religious Division	5	1	5.0	5.9
Drugs	6	1	5.0	5.9
One Parent Families	7	2	10.0	11.8
Catholic Church	8	1	5.0	5.9
Totals		20	100.0	117.6

TABLE 9:2 : TECHNOLOGICAL IMPACTS ON INTEGRATED EDUCATION (12 MISSING CASES - 12 VALID CASES)

Category Label	Code	Count	% of Responses	% of Cases
Internet	1	2	16.7	16.7
CLASP	2	1	8.3	8.3
I.T.	3	9	75.0	75.0
Totals		12	100.0	100.0

TABLE 9:3 : POLITICAL AND LEGAL IMPACTS ON
INTEGRATED EDUCATION
(10 MISSING CASES - 14 VALID CASES)

Category Label	Code	Count	% of Responses	% of Cases
Political climate	1	7	33.3	50.0
Govt. less anxious	2	2	9.5	14.3
Changes in attitudes	3	3	14.3	21.4
DENI constraints	4	2	9.5	14.3
Tribalism	5	1	4.8	7.1
Drumcree	6	2	9.5	14.3
UVF	7	1	4.8	7.1
Child Act	8	2	9.5	14.3
Code of Practice	9	1	4.8	7.1
Totals		21.0	100.0	150.0

TABLE 9:4 :ECONOMIC IMPACTS ON INTEGRATED
EDUCATION (7 MISSING CASES - 17 VALID CASES)

Category Label	Code	Count	% of Responses	% of Cases
Travel	1	3	15.0	17.6
No funds - DENI	2	10	50,0	58.8
No nursery funds	3	3	15.0	17.6
Societal influence	4	1	5.0	5.9
Funds for building	5	1	5.0	5.9
Cut back in music	6	1	5.0	5.9
Unemployment	7	1	5.0	5.9
Totals		20	100.0	117.6

TABLE 10:1 : STRENGTHS OF INTEGRATED
EDUCATION (3 MISSING CASES - 21 VALID CASES)

Category Label	Code	Count	% of Responses	% of Cases
Small team	1	18	38.3	85.7
Family atmosphere	2	3	6.4	14.3
Parental support	3	12	25.5	57.1
Caring environment	4	2	4.3	9.5
Educational standards	6	2	4.3	9.5
Positive attitude	7	1	2.1	4.8
Dedicated governors	8	4	8.5	19.0
Good community relations	9	5	10.6	23.8
Totals		47	100.0	223.8

TABLE 10:2 : WEAKNESSES OF INTEGRATED
EDUCATION (3 MISSING CASES - 21 VALID CASES)

Category Label	Code	Count	% of Responses	% of Cases
Lack of finance	1	5	17.2	23.8
Unsuitable buildings	2	9	31.0	42.9
Teaching staff	3	3	10.3	14.3
Poor facilities	4	5	17.2	23.8
Transport	5	2	6.9	9.5
New school	6	1	3.4	4.8
Negative influences	7	3	10.3	14.3
Ability to attract pupils	8	1	3.4	4.8
Totals		29	100.0	138.1

TABLE 10:3 : OPPORTUNITIES FOR INTEGRATED
EDUCATION (6 MISSING CASES - 18 VALID CASES)

Category Label	Code	Count	% of Responses	% of Cases
Change adult perceptions	1	4	13.8	22.2
New school	2	8	27.6	44.4
Staff development	3	3	10.3	16.7
Increase pupils	4	3	10.3	16.7
New class	5	1	3.4	5.6
Growth	6	10	34.5	55.6
Totals		29	100.0	161.6

TABLE 10:4 : THREATS FACING INTEGRATED
EDUCATION (3 MISSING CASES - 21 VALID CASES)

Category Label	Code	Count	% of Responses	% of Cases
Church	1	8	21.1	38.1
Vandalism	2	10	26.3	47.6
No funding	3	11	28.9	52.4
DENI funding	4	2	5.3	9.5
Closure if numbers fall	5	2	5.3	9.5
Rumours	6	1	2.6	4.8
Rural transport	7	2	5.3	9.5
Bigots	8	1	2.6	4.8
Turn pupils away	9	1	2.6	4.8
Totals		38	100.0	181.0

THE CURRENT CLIMATE

It would seem, therefore, that we have reached an important
watershed in the development of integrated schools in
Northern Ireland. While the legal and policy context is more

supportive than in the past, and the number of schools that have opened has, for all practical purposes, guaranteed the viability of the integrated sector, a question-mark remains over the future mode of growth in the sector. In addition, while the integrated sector exists, does it have a definite sectoral character, beyond religious headcounts, which might help in any expansion in the future, particularly if this expansion occurs through the transformation of existing schools rather than the development of entirely new ones?

The next factor for consideration is that of a contracting market. Even within the integrated sector the individual schools are very competitive with one another and this is reflected in some of the comments from the semi-structured interviews with the principals.

> Each school is perhaps like a little island with N.I.C.I.E. as another! Each school is concerned about its own agenda and does not really consider other schools or the overview of integrated education. Schools are preoccupied with their own agendas without considering the needs of others.

Even the umbrella body, NICIE, was not regarded as an integral part of the strategic marketing process as some of the principals declared during their interviews.

> N.I.C.I.E. are excellent at set-up but very poor in development. They (NICIE) have had their own problems with staff turnover and this hasn't helped the schools. Apart from an occasional social function I have not had the opportunity to meet the N.I.C.I.E. directors and don't feel they play a significant role.

The integrated sector faces the new millennium against a backdrop of intense competition from other schools, a reduction in government funding and a degree of apathy, by the general public, of the need for its development in the presence of a declared 'peace process.' The future remains uncertain.

NATIONAL IRISH BANK
COPING WITH A CRISIS AND BEYOND[1]

Gerry Mortimer

As March 1998 drew to a close, management at National Irish Bank (NIB) would have been forgiven for believing that the bank's situation could not get any worse. The bank had just issued a robust defence of its position in relation to an off shore bond scheme which had been the subject of much media and political debate for the previous two months. In particular, it had severely criticised RTE, the state owned television and radio corporation, and the two RTE journalists who had broken and dominated the story.

However, on March 25th, the same two journalists, Charlie Bird and George Lee, exposed a new damaging story on NIB. They claimed to have discovered that the bank had been overcharging interest and other charges on small businesses and personal accounts at 5 named branches of NIB. By mid morning, those branches, and others of NIB, were under siege by unhappy account holders and journalists.

At the corporate headquarters of NIB's parent, National Australia Bank (NAB), directors would soon become aware of yet another unwanted story involving its Irish subsidiary. In Ireland's booming economy, an apparently shrewd purchase of NIB by NAB in 1987 was looking increasingly sour.

ORIGINS OF NATIONAL IRISH BANK
National Irish Bank had been established as Northern Bank more than a century ago. As its name implied, it was a regional Irish bank which had most of its operations in the northern part of Ireland. When Ireland was partitioned in 1922, six northern counties had remained within the United Kingdom, while the remaining 26 counties became the Irish Free State

---

1 This case was developed as a basis for class discussion, rather than to illustrate either effective or ineffective handling of an administrative situation. It was developed from material in the public domain.

and, eventually, the Irish Republic. The bulk of Northern Bank's business was on the northern side of the new border, though the bank did have a presence in southern border counties such as Leitrim and Cavan. As these, and other, border counties were, for decades, among the most disadvantaged areas of the Irish Republic, Northern Bank was not a significant player south of the border. In Northern Ireland, it held a dominant position with an estimated 40% market share. The population of Northern Ireland, at 1.5 million, was less than half of that of the Irish Republic of 3.5 million. Northern Ireland was much more heavily industralised than the Republic with major industrial sectors in shipbuilding, engineering and textiles. The Irish Republic, with its agriculture dependent economy and high levels of emigration, would not have been seen as an attractive market by the Northern Bank, or its great rival, Ulster Bank.[2] In any event, several other regional banks dominated the banking sector on the rest of the island.

Huge changes swept through Ireland from the late fifties onwards. New policies were introduced to encourage economic growth. Foreign manufacturing industry was actively encouraged to establish in Ireland with capital and tax incentives. The 1966 Free Trade Agreement with the UK ended an era of protectionism which had been a cornerstone of Irish policy for more than 40 years. This agreement paved the way for the entry of Ireland, together with the UK and Denmark, to the European Community in 1973. While some traditional industries, which had prospered in the era of protectionism, suffered, the Irish economy grew rapidly throughout the sixties and early seventies. Emigration reduced considerably and, in fact, in several years, there was net migration into Ireland. Banks were not immune from this change. A series of mergers and takeovers in the banking sector during this time led to the creation of two major banking groups in the Irish Republic, Allied Irish Bank (AIB) and Bank of Ireland. Just as Northern Bank and Ulster Bank had limited presence in the Irish Republic, so

---

2 Ulster was, historically, Ireland's most northerly of four provinces. It comprised the six counties of Northern Ireland and three counties, Cavan, Monaghan and Donegal, which had become part of the Irish Republic in 1922.

also AIB and Bank of Ireland had limited presence in Northern Ireland. The economies of the two parts of the island operated almost totally independently of each other with relatively little trade between the two.

This was further underlined by the outbreak of conflict in Northern Ireland in 1969. This conflict, known as 'the troubles' was to last almost 30 years and would have a significant effect on the economy of Northern Ireland. With bank consolidation prevalent, both Northern Bank and Ulster Bank were taken over by larger UK based banks. Northern became part of the Midland Bank and Ulster became part of NatWest.

Ulster Bank had always had a larger presence than Northern in the Irish Republic with about 8% market share. Under its new parentage, Northern Bank set out to expand aggressively into the south. Its tactics of major expansion of the branch network to large cities and towns in the Republic and, in particular of targeting suitable sectors and accounts, horrified the rather complacent world of the existing larger players and were deemed in the early seventies as 'ungentlemanly' and 'not the done thing.'

Northern Bank succeeded, to some extent, in growing its share of the market in the Irish Republic though it never appeared to go higher than the current estimated level of 3%. However, in a market where margins were good, the economy was growing strongly and technology had yet to revolutionise the industry, it was possible to generate an acceptable return on investment with such a small share.

Two major recessions changed the situation totally. The first recession, in the mid seventies, was triggered by the international oil crisis, which hit all western economies. Ireland recovered strongly from that crisis but suffered again in the early eighties. The second recession also had its origins in an oil crisis. However, it was exacerbated by economic mismanagement and by a subsequent failure to deal with the root causes of that mismanagement. The Irish economy struggled through much of the eighties and early nineties before overcoming its problems and resuming rapid growth.

However, for Northern Bank's parent, Midland Bank, the Irish economy was a mere sideshow to its own problems. Midland had purchased a US based bank, Wells Fargo and had been experiencing serious financial difficulties as a result. In 1987 it began to offload businesses not seen as core. Among these were Northern Bank and Clydesdale Bank in Scotland.

National Australia Bank (NAB) purchased both and later added Yorkshire Bank, based in Northern England to its portfolio. This, and other surgery, failed to preserve Midland's independence and it was subsequently taken over by the Hong Kong and Shanghai Bank Corporation (HSBC).

National Australia Bank moved quickly to reorganise its Irish operations. It separated the Northern Ireland and Irish Republic operations with each reporting to corporate HQ. It renamed the Irish Republic operation National Irish Bank and appointed a new young chief executive, Jim Lacey. NAB had a reputation for adopting an aggressive marketing approach. This philosophy was to be passed on to NIB. Many senior managers in both Irish operations found the new approach difficult to accept and either left the banks, or retired, leaving largely new management teams in place.

THE DEVELOPMENT OF NATIONAL IRISH BANK

Jim Lacey and his management team set out to grow NIB's market share. It was the policy of its parent to seek a minimum of 10% share in any market in which it operated. NIB's relatively small size in the Irish market meant that it could not match the larger players in key financial ratios. Its return on assets was below 1% against the 1.15% to 1.25% of AIB and Bank of Ireland. Also its cost/income ratio was higher than most of its competitors again reflecting its high fixed cost base. The following table illustrates the positions of three of the small banks in 1994.

	NIB	**ULSTER**	**TSB**
Assets	£1100m	£3100m	£1230m
Pre Tax Profit	£14.6m	£62m	£15.1m
No of branches	57	98	72
Employment	823	1700	1100
Cost/income ratio	63%	57%	71%

NIB's options were to grow organically or through acquisition. It sought to achieve the former through a greater focus on business banking and through raising its profile. An example of the latter was its willingness to preempt or react quickest to any downward changes in interest rates announced by the Irish Central Bank. This usually afforded the bank valuable publicity. Acquisition possibilities began to emerge in the early nineties when the Irish government indicated that it might consider selling some or all of the banks which it controlled. The three banks effectively owned by the state, TSB, ACC Bank and ICC Bank, all had small market shares and were not considered to be viable in the longer term. TSB was an amalgamation of a number of smaller savings banks. ICC Bank and ACC Bank had been set up several decades earlier to provide long term credit for industrial and agricultural customers respectively. While all three banks had broadened their customer base in recent years, each still relied to some extent on their original niches of small savers, agriculture and industrial development. All three banks realised that they would need to develop new linkages. One of the options mooted was the merging of all three state banks to create what became known as 'the third force' after AIB and Bank of Ireland. TSB was keen on a link up with NIB while ACC Bank was proposing a takeover by an overseas bank, possibly Credit Agricole, one of the largest banks in France.

NIB entered a due diligence process with TSB and subsequently made an offer in excess of £100 million for TSB. Ulster bank indicated a willingness to exceed NIB's offer subject to due diligence. NIB raised its offer to £125 m and seemed certain to takeover TSB. Suddenly, and without apparent warning, NIB dismissed Jim Lacy in 1994. Lacy had come to general public notice in 1993 when he was kidnapped and held for ransom. He faught the dismissal but eventually settled for a substantial payment believed to be in the region of £750,000 and resigned his position. It was speculated that the new merged bank was to be headed not by Lacy but by the Chief Executive of TSB and that this had precipitated the decision to dismiss Lacy. The government of the day stalled on the sale of TSB and commissioned reports to look at the options for all three state banks. No conclusions had been reached by the time the government fell in 1995. The new government was less disposed towards a sell off of state assets and little progress of substance was made. All three banks in the control or ownership of the state were improving their results, due principally to a booming economy. By 1998, each would have increased in value due to improved profitability and a higher P/E rating for bank shares generally. NIB, and its parent company, NAB, regularly expressed its frustration at the slow pace of developments. However, in January 1998, NIB began to make headlines for all the wrong reasons.

THE FIRST CRISIS

Early in January, the two RTE reporters broke a story that NIB had sold offshore bonds operated by Clerical Medical International in the tax haven of the Isle of Man. It appeared that existing NIB customers were targeted for the bonds by the NIB salesforce.

The clear inference was that the customers were seeking to evade tax on their investment. The source of the money used to purchase the bonds might also be questioned though that would be a matter between the customer and the Irish tax authorities. There was also some indication that customers retained some access to their funds through NIB. A total of £50m was believed to have been involved with several hundred different accounts. The story ran over several days and was deeply embarrassing for NIB. The story developed additional newsworthiness when it emerged that a key NIB employee involved was Beverly Cooper-Flynn. Ms Cooper-Flynn had resigned from the bank having been elected as a member of parliament in 1997. She was the daughter of Padraig Flynn a well known, colourful and, sometimes controversial, politician. Mr Flynn had resigned his government positions and his parliamentary seat in 1994 when appointed a Commissioner of the European Community. His daughter had failed to win the subsequent by election but had been elected at the next general election in 1997. The Chief Executive of TSB was reported as saying that there would now be no deal with NIB.

The government established an enquiry into the circumstances of the bonds sale. In fact, by March, there were four formal enquiries taking place. The Central Bank of Ireland, the

Irish Tax Authorities, the Government Department of Enterprise and Employment and NAB's European Audit team, were all investigating the NIB 'scandal' as it became known. These had only commenced their work when the second crisis hit NIB. Angered by the constant drip feed of allegations arising from the bonds sale, NIB issued a statement on March 24th which was highly critical of RTE and the two reporters principally involved. In it they accused the reporters and RTE of dealing in stolen internal documents. NIB employed one of the country's leading consultancy firms on an ongoing basis. There is no evidence that the PR agency was involved. However in view of earlier press releases it seems unlikely that the PR agency would not, at least, have been consulted. The following extract illustrates the bank's position.

'Our own investigations had found areas which gave rise to concern. However, sweeping generalisations made against the bank, on the basis of selective information, had not been substantiated. The bank had been pilloried and harassed by RTE on an almost daily basis'

Far from being dissuaded from further coverage of the story, the reporters turned their attention to a different issue and on a television current affairs programme, Prime Time on March 25th they made new and damaging allegations against NIB.

THE SECOND CRISIS

As previously noted, this centred on a claim that NIB managers in five separate branches had loaded additional interest on customers' accounts without their knowledge. It was claimed that internal audits had discovered the practice which covered much of the late eighties and early nineties. The practice was stopped at the insistence of senior management in NIB including, apparently, the then Chief Executive, Jim Lacey. However, no staff were disciplined and no money was refunded to those affected.

The story immediately received wide coverage in all media. The coverage was highly critical of NIB. Politicians and media called for enquiries into the operation of the bank. An emergency government cabinet meeting was held. A statement was issued expressing 'grave concern' and promising use of 'appropriate powers' of the state. It was claimed that the policy of loading interest was motivated by pressure from senior managers on branch managers to grow their business and improve fee income. It was apparent that one or more ex-employees of NIB was being used as a source by RTE for its allegations and that it had documents to support its case.

NATIONAL AUSTRALIA BANK

NAB is the largest bank in Australia with an estimated market share in that country of 20%. It has its headquarters in Melbourne. It has extensive overseas interests which account for more than 50% of its assets. Outside Australia, its principal areas of activity are in the midwest and southwest of the USA where it owns a number of small banks and mortgage corporations. It also has Asian interests and owns a bank in New Zealand. In Europe, its major interests are in UK and Ireland. As previously noted, in the UK it owns Clydesdale Bank in Scotland, Yorkshire Bank in England and Northern Bank in Northern Ireland. Each is a traditional branch based bank. None of its UK subsidiaries held substantial market share in the UK as a whole though each was strong in its region. Overall in its most recent financial year NAB reported net profits of IR£1000million. NIB reported profits of £16million for the same period. NAB is approximately double the size of Ireland's largest bank, AIB.

THE IRISH BANKING MARKET IN 1998

The two major banks in Ireland, AIB and Bank of Ireland, continued to dominate the Irish banking market as they had done for several decades. Both were independent concerns quoted on Dublin and London Stock Exchanges. AIB was the larger, with an estimated value of IR£8 billion as against IR£6 billion for Bank of Ireland. However, Bank of Ireland was slightly larger in an Irish Republic Market context. For example its share of the current account market in 1997 was 42% against 37% for AIB. Similarly its share of the bank savings account market was at 44% against 41% for AIB. These indicators probably reflected overall share in the banking sector with Bank of Ireland just above 40% and AIB just below.

AIB's greater capitalisation reflected its more important interests outside the Irish Republic. AIB had 20% market share in Northern Ireland with its subsidiary, First Trust, which was an amalgamation of its own small branch network and its purchase of the Northern Ireland Trustee Savings Bank. AIB also had a small presence in the rest of the UK and a controlling interest in a bank in Poland. However, its major overseas interest was its ownership of First Maryland Bank in the US. This purchase and subsequent other purchases in the same region had resulted in AIB owning a substantial and successful regional bank which contributed a significant proportion of AIB's overall profit. Overall some 60% of AIB's net profit of £580m in 1997 was earned outside the Irish Republic.

Bank of Ireland also possessed overseas interests though these were less extensive. It had, relatively recently, purchased the Bristol and West Building Society in the UK for some £600m. It also had branch interests in the UK. It had also followed AIB into the US market though with much less success. It had concentrated its efforts in New Hampshire, purchasing a bank there in the eighties. It had expended large sums to stem major losses there and had eventually sold most of its interest retaining only a minority share.

Ulster bank was in third position in the Irish market with an estimated market share of about 8%. In what was regarded as the traditional banking sector, remaining market share was held by NIB, TSB, ICC, ACC and Anglo Irish each with 2-3% of the market. As previously noted only NIB could be seen as competing in all sectors of the industry. TSB largely offered services to consumers at the less affluent end of the market. This is reflected in its estimated share of 10% of savings accounts in the bank sector and 7% of current (checkbook) accounts as compared to its overall share of less than 3%. Share was determined by the total volume of business.

ICC Bank and Anglo Irish Bank focussed mainly on smaller businesses. ACC Bank had developed as a provider of finance to the farming and agri-business sectors, though in recent years, it had developed into a broader based bank.

Clearly, the traditional banking sector could not be viewed in isolation. Many of the services provided by Irish banks were also provided by other types of institutions. For example, in a survey by MRBI for Irish Permanent, it was established that 38% of the population aged 15+ held a savings account with a credit union. Credit unions, which were non profit organisations typically based around a geographical area, employment type or place of work, offered both savings and loan facilities. Normally, the amount one could borrow from a credit union was closely related to one's savings record. There were several hundred credit unions in Ireland. They had developed rapidly in recent years and had come together under an umbrella group, Irish League of Credit Unions. Together, they had, assets in excess of £2.6billion, more than double those of NIB. New legislation in 1997 had allowed credit unions greater freedom to operate and had caused concerns for existing banks which considered that there was unfair favourable treatment for credit unions, particularly in the area of tax treatment of deposits. Another major sector was that of building societies. These had been established as mutual organisations, mostly in the 19th century, comprised of groups which had formed to provide long term finance for house purchase. Ireland had the second highest rate of home ownership in the developed world with only New Zealand having a higher rate. Change had also come to the building society sector in recent years. Of the major societies, Irish Permanent, the largest, had already demutualised and was now a quoted PLC. ICS Building Society was effectively controlled by Bank of Ireland. Of the other three societies of any significance, First National had already announced its intention to demutualise in 1998. Irish Nationwide was known to be interested in changing its status but realised that it was probably not of sufficient size to go the PLC route alone. However, legislation which allowed demutualisation, also prohibited any one shareholder from owning more than 15% of a new PLC for five years after demutualisation. The principal arguments in favour of demutualisation were access to new capital and the ability to compete more directly with banks on a broader basis.

EBS was the only major building socieity which had deliberately and publicly opted to remain mutual. It argued that its very mutuality benefited both its savers and its borrowers as it did not have shareholders to serve.

All the current or demutualised building societies operated an extensive network of, mostly, small branches and agencies

throughout the country with the exception of ICS which
appeared to becoming more directly absorbed into Bank of
Ireland.

The principal activities of these branches were for handling
of savings accounts and the issuing of mortgages. Increasingly
the latter was being undertaken by phone and through the
head office. Most building societies had cooperated in recent
years with the establishment of ATMs which recognised each
others customers cards. The share of the Irish mortgage market based on a MRBI survey is illustrated below. Banks had,
increasingly, entered this market and developed significant
share in recent years.

	Market share %
Irish Permanent	21
Bank of Ireland/ICS	17
AIB	14
First National	14
EBS Building Society	11
Irish Nationwide Building Society	6
TSB	3
Irish Life Assurance Co	3
NIB	2
ACC Bank	2
Others	7

Telephone banking had made some limited inroads on the Irish
market. However, in virtually all cases, the businesses had
been established by existing players in the market. The first,
and still most important, was Premier Banking, which had
been developed by Bank of Ireland. It was deemed a success,
due to its low cost base. However its market share was small.

Thus it can be seen that the Irish banking market continued
to be dominated by the well established players offering their
services through traditional routes though the ways in which
customers accessed their banking facilities were moving towards
more electronic methods. Banks were keen to encourage this
trend as it was recognised that provision of face to face high
street branch services was expensive. Whether such change
would be evolutionary or revolutionary remained to be seen.

THE IRISH ECONOMY IN 1998

The Irish economy had boomed through much of the nineties. Industrial output had doubled between 1992 and 1998. Economic growth as measured by Gross National Product (GNP) and Gross Domestic Product (GDP) had reached and sustained unprecedented levels. GNP was regarded as the more accurate of the two measures as it factored out repatriation of profit by multinational corporations. GNP had grown by 8.3% in 1996, 7.7% in 1997 and was confidently forecast to grow by up to 10% in 1998. These growth rates were considered unsustainable in the longer term without inducing major inflationary pressures. However it was regarded as remarkable that the economy had grown strongly for several years without experiencing significant upward pressure on inflation. Ireland had comfortably met the criteria for entry into the new single currency for the European Union which would come into effect at the beginning of 1999. These criteria related to the following:

- Inflation rates 'an average rate of inflation...that does not exceed by more than 1.5 percentage points that of, at most, the three best performing Member States in terms of price stability;'
- Interest rates: 'a Member State has had an average nominal long-term interest rate that does not exceed by more than two percentage points that of, at most, the three best performing Member States in terms of price stability;'
- Exchange rates: 'the observance of the normal fluctuation margins provided for by the exchange-rate mechanism of the European Monetary System, for at least two years, without devaluing against the currency of any other Member State';
- 'the sustainability of the government financial position'. As judged by the following two measures:

    Budget deficit: 'the ratio of the planned or actual government deficit to gross domestic product at market prices' cannot exceed '3%'.

    National debt: 'the ratio of government debt to gross domestic product at market prices' cannot exceed '60%'.

SOURCE: MAASTRICHT TREATY as cited in Principles of Economics by Turley and Maloney

The one criterion which was causing some concern was Irish inflation, which, though below 3%, was beginning to drift upwards relative to the criteria used.

Ireland would join the new currency union with 10 other European Union members. The other members would be France, Germany, Italy, Belgium, Holland, Luxembourg, Spain, Italy, Austria and Portugal. UK, Sweden and Denmark had opted not to join in the short term, while Greece was not deemed to have met the criteria. The single currency, the Euro, would replace all participating currencies by 2002.

Ireland's fast growing economy was driven by two major factors. One of these was the growth in exports of multinationals. The top 20 exporters accounted for 36% of Irish exports which in turn accounted for 80% of Irish GNP. Of the top 20, 10 are multinationals, while the remainder are long established food and drink companies.

The second major factor was the dramatic growth in the service economy. This was also fuelled by MNCs in financial services and call centres and by the growth in tourism.

The growth was made possible also by demographic factors. There had been a large population bulge in the sixties and seventies and this group were now swelling the labour market. A high proportion were well educated and suited to employment in the growth sectors. There was also a major increase in women reentering the workforce. Now, with a falling child population and a rapidly growing workforce, Ireland's dependency ratio was the lowest in Europe. Unlike other European countries it was still falling and was not expected to level out until well into the next century. This suggested that the Irish economy could still grow relatively rapidly for the next several years. In the long term, economists were indicating potential GNP growth of 5% arising from an annual 2% growth in the workforce and a 3% growth in productivity.

Inevitably, due to the openness of the Irish economy, it would be subject to external changes. The Irish economy was relatively insulated from direct involvement with growing economic problems in Asia. However, problems in Europe or the US could have a significant impact. Closer to home, Ireland continued to rely to an important, though declining, extent on trade with the UK. The UK took over 20% of Irish exports and a much higher proportion of indigenous exports. The UK currency, sterling, had been very strong of late and in March 1998 stood at a 5 year high of about Ir£1=£0.85Stg. Sterling had been at a low of Ir£1=£1.10 Stg. during that 5 year period. Irish exporters were benefitting greatly from the high value of sterling. As previously noted, UK was not participating in European monetary union and sterling would continue to float against the new Euro after January 1999. However, as will be illustrated below, the arrival of the Euro would have significant effects on the profits of Irish banks.

IRISH BANKING AND THE FUTURE
There were a number of major factors likely to effect the operations of Irish banks in the future. These can be summarised under a number of headings.

Technology
It is clear that technology is a key factor. Developments such as Internet banking and computer telephoning integration can greatly improve access and services to customers. Such developments can have a global reach and can also reduce or eliminate the need for a local physical presence in each market. It could also facilitate the entry of new low cost providers.

New Forms of Competition
The Irish banking market has remained, largely, the same for decades. There has been some blurring at the edges. However most of this has resulted from the major banks offering other services rather than other service providers entering banking. For example, each of the two largest banks, AIB and B of I have established life assurance subsidiaries, each of which has become a significant player in the Irish market. On the other hand, no assurance company has developed any presence in the banking market. Irish Life, the largest life assurance company in Ireland, has shown interest in some of the smaller banks, particularly since the appointment of a new chief executive who had been previously chief executive of Ulster Bank. This contrasts with the developments in the UK market where the blurring of offerings between service providers has widened the market considerably. This is illustrated in the table shown in

the appendix. Extracted from the Time newspaper, it illustrates the response to a phone request to 19 banks and building societies asking to deposit £1000. Of the 19, Tesco, Safeway
and Sainsbury are all banks owned and operated by supermar-
ket groups. Egg has recently been established by Prudential
Assurance. Standard Life is also an assurance company.
Halifax, C & G, Britannia and Woolwich are all originally
building societies, which have demutualised. Bristol and West
is owned by Bank of Ireland and Yorkshire owned by NAB. The
traditional 'big 4' clearing banks are Barclays, Midland, Nat
West and Lloyds TSB. Nationwide and Bradford and Bingley
continued as building societies though they were under pressure to demutualise.

Other evidence of widening competition is illustrated by the
recent arrival in Ireland of MBNA. It is one of the largest credit card providers in the world and concentrates exclusively on
that sector. This sector, in Ireland, has, hitherto, been the presence of the main banks.

European Monetary Union
The arrival of the Euro in 1999 will significantly affect the
banking sector. It will, for example, eliminate bank profits from
trading in many currencies. The individual currencies will, in
any event, disappear in 2002. However, in the meantime,
banks have been instructed to offer standard full rates on currency exchange. Thus Ir£1 will equal 2.48dms. It has been
estimated that some banks could lose up to 10% of their profits
as a result of the change. For Irish banks the effect may be less
serious in the short term give that the UK is not joining.
However, pressure to price products in Euros in the UK may
become overwhelming. In any event, the UK may join in the
future.

The other major effect of the Euro is likely to be on interest
rates and the availability of loans. By definition, interest rates
will have to converge in the new system. While there may still
be variations for small loans and deposits depending on such
factors as risk, customers, particularly larger customers, will
be in a position to shop around for the best deal. Traditionally,
margins (the difference between the average rate of interest
charged and paid by a bank) have been higher in Ireland,

though they have been narrowing in recent years. European banks have always operated on lower margins. Typical average margins might be in the range of 1.5% to 2.5%. Margins on smaller loans and those with a perceived higher risk tend to be higher. There was much discussion taking place about likely consolidation of the estimated 14,000 banks in Europe.

National Irish Bank would be National Australia Bank's only subsidiary in the Euro Zone. As the unfavourable media coverage continued apace at the end of March 1998, it was clear that both short and long term decisions would need to be taken by National Irish Bank and by its parent, National Australia Bank.

APPENDIX

SHOPPING AROUND FOR A BETTER SAVINGS SERVICE

* on instant access

		Number of rings	Wait in queue	Man or machine	% rate for deposit of £1000*	What they call you	Level of service	Quality of advice	
Tesco	0345 104010	1	–	machine	6.75	–			Friendly and efficient
Safeway	0800 995 995	1	–	machine	7.5	–			Cold but helpful
Sainsbury's	0500 405 060	1	–	person	6.75	Madam			Friendly but not familiar
Egg	0845 0399 399	1	–	machine	8/7.5	–			A very cheerful machine recording
Standard Life	0345 555 657	2	–	person	7.35	–			Efficient and warm
Halifax	0345 263 646	2	–	person	n/a	–			Went out of his way to help
Nationwide	0500 302010	1	–	person	7.4	–			Friendly
C&G	0800 742 437	6	1 min	person	7.5	–			Honest – mentioned rates under review
Bradford & Bingley	0345 248 248	1	–	person	7.05	–			Had all the facts at their fingertips
Bristol & West	0800 202 121	1	–	person	n/a	–			Groaned when size of deposit mentioned
Britannia	0800 132 304	7	–	person	6.25	Ms Emmett			Keen to praise benefits of mutuality
Woolwich	0800 222 200	1	–	machine	6.75	–			No access to any information
Yorkshire Bank	0113 247 2 000	4	–	person	3.65	Luv			Branch only open 9am - 3.30pm
Barclays	0800 400 100	1	–	machine	4.0	–			Business-like and formal
Midland	0800 180 180	1	–	person	4.5	Susan			Got the rate wrong
Nat West	0800 505 050	5	7 mins	person	3.85	–			Laughed at size of deposit
Lloyds TSB	0800 147 789	14	6 mins	person	3.1	–			Well informed and friendly
RBS	0800 880 880	1	–	person	3.85	–			Admitted rate very low
Co-op	0345 252 000	8	3.5 mins	person	5.0	–			Stuck rigidly to prepared text

KEY: 🏧 Answered by machine 🧍 Answered by person   ☺ Excellent 😐 Average 🙁 Could improve 😫 Dreadful

Source: Times

WATERFORD CRYSTAL
THE CHAIRMAN'S CHALLENGE[1]

Gerry Mortimer

As he eased his car out the gates of Castlemartin on a lovely evening in May 1995, Redmond O'Donoghue mused on the meeting which had just finished. Dr A.J.F. O'Reilly, non executive Chairman of Waterford Wedgwood Plc, had brought senior management of the group to his Irish residence in County Kildare for an informal discussion on future strategy. The group comprised two distinct major subsidiaries, Waterford Crystal which produced crystal glass and Josiah Wedgwood whose main business was ceramic tableware. Redmond was Chief Operating officer of Waterford Crystal. With the impending retirement of the current Chief Executive, Paddy Galvin, Redmond was likely to succeed him as Chief Executive and so would have overall responsibility for developing and implementing future strategy for Waterford Crystal. Not for the first time, Redmond marvelled at the ability of the Chairman to get his key executives to "raise the bar" in committing themselves to ambitious objectives. Redmond had, at the meeting, proposed that Waterford Crystal should consider setting itself the target of doubling turnover and profit in the five years to the end of the decade. They had agreed to meet again in August and to finalise plans by the year end. He still had time to back off and develop less ambitious targets though, somehow, he doubted if the Chairman would be impressed! Waterford Crystal had successfully come through a period of several years of troubled trading which had almost brought the company to its knees. It was time to draw a line under the past and move forward. He was sure that senior executives in Waterford would relish the challenge to achieve the targets involved. On

---

1 This case was developed as a basis for class discussion, rather than to illustrate either effective or ineffective handling of an administrative situation. It was developed from material in the public domain.

the other hand, the immense scale of the challenge was apparent when he reflected on Waterford's core business. 75% of Waterford's business was the sale of crystal gift/tableware in the USA and a further 10% was to US visitors to Ireland. In all Waterford held an estimated just below 40% of the US premium cut crystal market. This market was highly mature with sales increasing at about 2% per annum. He recalled, from his time working with the Ford Motor Corporation, a competitive award called "the Chairman's Challenge." Truly, he thought, this surely was a real "Chairman's Challenge."

THE ORIGINS OF WATERFORD CRYSTAL

The production of crystal glass in Europe in the middle ages centred in Venice and gradually developed throughout Europe as Italian glass workers migrated to other countries. Bottle and table glass is recorded as having been produced in Waterford in the late 16th and early 17th centuries. One John Head of Waterford advertised in 1729 that he produced heavy and lightweight flint (crystal) drinking glasses. The first half of the 18th century saw a major development of Irish glass production with the key skills of blowing, cutting, engraving, moulding and enamel work being refined. During the 18th and 19th centuries changes in trade and tax laws in England and elsewhere greatly influenced the development of industries. For example, in 1746, an act in the English Parliament prohibited the export of Irish glass to England. This had a serious effect on the Irish industry. The situation was reversed some thirty years later when England imposed severe taxes on its producers and Ireland embraced free trade. Many English tradesmen migrated to Ireland and established glass manufacturing businesses there. This was apparently regarded as the golden age of Irish glass with designs becoming more elaborate. Exports became important and were shipped to Europe and North America. Irish designs were much copied abroad. Proximity to a port became an important issue in the glass business and Waterford, as the major port in the south east of Ireland with access to both England and continental Europe, was seen as a natural base for glass making. The most notable business in Waterford was established by the Penrose family which employed up to 70 people and was known as Waterford Flint

Glass. The business changed ownership on a few occasions. One such change, coupled with some gentle promotion, was announced in the Waterford Chronicle in December 1799 as follows:

> Ramsey, Gatchell and Barcroft respectfully inform their friends and the public that they have purchased the establishment of the Waterford Flint Glass manufactory from George and William Penrose and have opened a shop on the Quay in said concern where they intend to be supplied with an extensive assortment of plain and ornamental glassware and hope by their attention, moderate prices and the quality of their glass, to merit the approbation of their customers.

In reading this one can only conclude that the bases for sustainable competitive advantage have altered little in 200 years and were not invented by McCarthy, Kotler, Porter et al!

The 19th century was less kind to businesses such as Waterford Flint Glass. The Act of Union with Britain in 1801 ended Ireland's political and economic independence. Subsequent punitive tax laws appear to have been a major factor in the gradual decline of the company. Although the company apparently sent an outstanding entry to the Great Exhibition in London's Crystal Palace in 1851, it closed the same year.

THE MODERN WATERFORD CRYSTAL

A number of attempts were made to revive the business subsequently. However, it was not until 1947, almost a century later, that a new Waterford Glass business was established. A number of skilled craftsmen from central Europe were recruited. The designs from Waterford based glass companies of the eighteenth and nineteenth centuries were closely examined by the craftsmen. The designs of the new company were based, largely, on those earlier designs. The new company manufactured a range of lead crystal products. The principal ingredients of lead crystal are silica sand, litharge, which provides the lead content, and potassium carbonate. Typically, the ingredients are heated in a furnace. The raw material is then extracted from the furnace manually or automatically, and then blown and shaped, before being cooled and prepared for cutting. Crystal products can also be produced from blanks or pieces of solid crystal. Many smaller producers, who could not justify the investment in a furnace, purchase blanks and complete the process from there. The higher the lead content, the greater the sparkle and light refraction. Waterford Glass, subsequently renamed as Waterford Crystal, has consistently produced crystal with a lead content in excess of 30%. Cheaper products use a lower lead content. Waterford struggled for several years, first making a profit in 1955. From that point, the company grew rapidly. It went public in 1966 when it obtained a share listing in the Dublin and London Stock Exchanges. Subsequently, it acquired Josiah Wedgwood, a well known, UK based, ceramic tableware company, in 1985. The acquisition had a certain logic to it. The companies operated in complementary areas and offered possible synergies in marketing and distribution. The eighties were a period of rapid expansion for Waterford as the US market boomed in the Reagan era. The product range also expanded to encompass a huge range of gift and tableware totalling up to 4000 separate items, recorded as stock keeping units or SKUs. The key distinguishing features of Waterford Crystal were the heavy and angular cut to the glass. The company was very reliant on the US market where Waterford was a strong market leader and a brand name of major importance. All Waterford Crystal was mouth blown and hand cut. No seconds were permitted to leave the factory. Products which did not reach the required standard were destroyed with a proportion of usable glass returned to the furnace.

The decline in the fortunes of Waterford Crystal, in the late eighties, was sudden and precipitous. The US market experienced a recession. Luxury goods, as one might expect, were not immune from this. Waterford had been used to consistent growth. High inflation and low dollar values also contributed to its problems. The company was forced to abandon some price points in the premium crystal market and the vacated market segments were occupied by competitors. From 1987 onwards the company began to make severe losses. Its problems were compounded by two key factors. The company was low technology in an industry where advanced technology was becoming readily available, particularly in cutting and blowing, which were now possible using automated equipment. Over the years, the company had experienced significant wage cost drift. Work practices, which inhibited efficiency, had become established. In 1989, a new management team was appointed to a company which was losing £20 million per annum on a turnover which was falling rapidly, reaching a low point of £73 million in 1991. New institutional and private investors, such as Morgan Stanley and Dr O'Reilly acquired significant share holdings in the company in 1990 and saw the value of their investment fall as the company struggled to overcome its difficulties.

As an illustration of the difficulties involved, US sales dropped by one third in 1991. Recent sales and profit figures for Waterford Crystal and Josiah Wedgwood are shown in the table below:

WATERFORD CRYSTAL   JOSIAH WEDGWOOD

	Sales	Net Profit	Sales	Net Profit
1995	120	15	220	17
1994	108.8	13	216.2	15.3
1993	102.1	7.8	217.1	8.7
1992	76.3	0.5	197.3	8.6
1991	73	(1.2)	219.1	10.3
1990	76.7	(4.8)	231.2	14.8
1989	95.8	N/A	251.6	N/A

All figures in IR£M

Note: The company did not report separate profit figures for the two divisions in 1989. The group, as a whole, returned a loss of £1.1M.

Source: Waterford Wedgwood Annual Reports

THE TURNAROUND

The changes introduced by the new management were radical. As articulated by the then Chairman and Chief Executive of Waterford Crystal, Paddy Galvin, the strategy adopted was twofold:

1.   Develop a turnaround strategy simply to survive
2.   Develop a new strategy for growth

Much of the first element was cost driven. 800 staff, or one-third of the work force in Waterford was shed over four years. Wages and salary rates were cut by up to 25% and a pay freeze was imposed to the end of 1994. Major advances were made in productivity and changed work practices. These were strongly resisted, but eventually embraced, by the workforce. Major improvements were instituted in industrial relations and the management, staff and unions worked closely together to move the company forward, once the initial problems were overcome. The company introduced an internal communications programme to ensure that all staff were kept fully informed of important developments. Almost as radical was a decision to source the manufacture of certain products out of Waterford and Ireland. This was seen at the time as having possible serious consequences for the Waterford based operation. It raised much discussion on the relationship of the city and the brand. It was particularly controversial in Ireland, where Waterford Crystal was seen as having a symbiotic relationship with the nation and with Waterford City and County in particular. Whether customers understood or appreciated this symbiosis is open to some doubt.

The new strategy for growth was, itself, comprised of a number of major elements. The existing range was revamped to cover a wider span of the premium crystal market. This was done while at the same time reducing the number of stock keeping units to 2000. Of these, about 600 accounted for 80% of sales. While drinking glasses, in a wide variety of designs and uses, made up the largest product category, the range also included other crystal tableware, dishes, bowls, ornaments, clocks, lighting ware and trophies. Any item which could be produced in crystal and cut in one of the many elaborate styles developed by Waterford was considered for production. A second element was the redevelopment of the visitor centre at the main Waterford plant. A total of £1.5m was spent on revamping and extending the visitor centre. The new centre enables visitors to walk through the factory to see the various operations in a logical sequence (and to smash rejected products if they wish). A restaurant, audio visual area and information centre were also added. The Waterford Crystal Gallery, which displays the product range and is also a retail outlet, was extended. In 1992, just over 100,000 visitors came to the centre. By 1995 this figure was approaching 250,000 and continuing to grow. It was then the fourth biggest tourist attraction in Ireland for overseas visitors. An estimated 50% of all visitors purchase some crystal.

The most radical strategy change was the development of a new crystal product range aimed principally at the US market. This was branded as *"Marquis by Waterford Crystal". It was designed to sell at a lower price than Waterford but with higher margins. These higher margins were achieved through outsourcing the product in Germany, where advanced technology reduced the cost of the product, and Slovenia, which offered considerably lower labour costs. In using new technologies, Marquis moved Waterford away from its previous policy of 100% mouth blown and hand cut. Marquis was lighter in feel, design and cut and was targeted at a younger market. It had its own packaging, advertising and identity. It was intended that it would obtain shelf space away from Waterford in retail outlets. A key objective was that Marquis would not cannibalise Waterford sales particularly in the vital US market. This was clearly achieved to a remarkable extent. By 1995 Marquis share of the US crystal market was approaching 10%. It was the fourth best selling brand in the market out of an estimated total of 120 brands. The Waterford brand maintained its number one position in the market. Indeed its share of the US market grew from 23.5% in 1991, before the launch of Marquis, to an estimated 30% in 1995. Added together, the share of the US premium crystal market held by the company now amounted to some 40%.

The development of the Marquis brand and its rationale is fully described in "Marquis by Waterford: Creating a New International Brand" by Redmond O'Donoghue in Irish Marketing Review Volume 7, 1994 published by Mercury Publications, Dublin and reprinted in "Marketing in Action, Learning from a Small Country" edited by Aidan O'Driscoll and published by Mercury Publications in 1997.

An excellent example of innovative product development under the Waterford brand was a specially boxed pair of tall slender glasses described as Millennium Toasting Flutes launched in 1995. It is intended that a pair will be launched each year until the millennium with themes of happiness, love, health, prosperity and peace. This product, retailing at $99 per pair, immediately became Waterford's best selling product in the US with sales heading towards 250,000 pairs per annum. Consumers were encouraged to complete the set by purchasing a pair each year.

WATERFORD CRYSTAL IN 1995

By 1995 the process of recovery was complete in Waterford Crystal. Turnover for the year was expected to amount to £120 million and net profit was expected to reach £15 million. These would be the figures on which the Chairman's Challenge would be based. Wedgwood sales were approximately £100 million more than Waterford though the difference in profitability was much less with Wedgwood profits 15% ahead of Waterford. Major advances in technology had also taken place at the Waterford premises. A new automated tank furnace costing about £10 million was being installed. The new plant improved the quality and clarity of the glass. The less cutting which was undertaken on a piece of glass, the more the quality of the crystal became under scrutiny. Extensive cutting could remove any flaws in the crystal and may even have been a factor in the choice of heavy cutting in both the original 18/19th century Waterford operation and the revived business when it commenced in 1947. It also enabled high technology blowing, cutting and forming. For example, long stemmed products, which could not be produced with previous technology, were now possible. Waterford was conscious of its craft heritage but recognised that it would have to embrace the new technologies available. The new plant offered greater options to Waterford Crystal but Redmond O'Donoghue and his team were conscious that the market appreciated the mouthblown and handcut features of the Waterford brand. Marquis had, however, proved that it was possible to market products which did not necessarily have either of those features.

The US market had recovered strongly. This was both a function of Waterford's strategy and of greatly improved economic conditions. Waterford was strongly focused on Anglophone markets. The USA, UK and Ireland accounted for 94% of sales. Other markets such as West Indies, Australia and Canada accounted for much of the rest.

In the key markets, Waterford obviously faced competition. In Ireland, this was limited to a range of small producers, many of whom had been inspired to develop by Waterford's success. Many had experienced trading difficulties and had operated under several ownerships. Companies included Galway, Cavan, Dublin, Tipperary as well as a large number of small regional or local producers. With the exception of Galway Crystal, none of the Irish based companies employed more than 100 employees and many were considerably smaller. Galway, which had been established in the seventies had, ironically, once been owned by Josiah Wedgwood. It was currently owned by the same investment company which owned Belleek China. While both had a reasonable level of market recognition, and sold into the key US market, neither was more than a fraction of the size of Waterford. No Irish based competitors were positioned directly against Waterford. Most operated at lower price points and many produced machine cut crystal with a lower lead content.

In the UK, Waterford was not the market leader. In fact, in 1994, it ranked at No. 5 in the market. The market, at wholesale prices, was valued at about £55m sterling (£1stg=£IR1). Estimated market shares are shown in the following table:

UK Market Shares in Crystal Market 1994	
Edinburgh	23%
Dartington	15%
Stuart	14%
Doulton	11%
Royal Brierley	9%
Waterford	8%
Lalique	1%
Others	19%

Source: Company Information

All the major competitors were UK owned. In May 1995, Waterford was considering purchasing the troubled Stuart Crystal. Edinburgh, the market leader, operated a chain of retail outlets while most of the other major players were principally in the china market.

In the US, as previously noted, Waterford ranked as the number one selling brand and Marquis was fourth. Again, actual figures for 1994 are shown below. As Waterford's overall share was continuing to rise in 1995, figures quoted elsewhere for Waterford products are not directly comparable.

US Market Share in Crystal Market 1994	
Waterford	27.5%
Mikasa	25.2%
Gorham	12.8%
Marquis	6.5%
Lenox	6.4%
Noritake	3.6%
Others	18.0%

Source: Company Information

Waterford considered, as competitors, those products which were positioned against them, in particular where they were sold on the same floor in department stores. However, Mikasa products typically retailed at 50% of equivalent Waterford prices while the other major competitors were approximately 75% of Waterford's price and close to Marquis prices. Lenox had been the major loser from the growth of Marquis. Both Lenox and Gorham were owned by Brown Forman whose major products were alcoholic beverages such as Southern Comfort and Jack Daniels. The two crystal companies were purchased by Brown Forman as part of a diversification strategy. Both were also prominent in china with each having at least 50% of its sales in that market. Lenox was largely only in stemware. Mikasa did not manufacture. Rather it outsourced all its product, principally in the Far East and Central Europe. Noritake was part of a very large Japanese owned tableware organisation. Most of the other products in the US market were imported from countries such as Sweden, France, Japan and the Czech Republic. Other Irish producers barely rated a mention in market share.

A key consideration in the coming together of Waterford and Wedgwood was the relative geographic strengths of both companies. Wedgwood was a strong presence in far eastern markets particularly Japan and Australia but was less prominent, though growing, in the USA. The position was largely reversed for Waterford. As a result Wedgwood handled Waterford distribution in markets where it had been strong while Waterford distributed Wedgwood products in the US.

The Waterford Crystal management team recognised the value of its strong market position in the US and were naturally concerned to maximise the strength of the brand in the US. Equally they were aware of the effects that the recession in the US had had on Waterford Crystal a few years previously.

While the US, Ireland and UK accounted for more than 90% of sales, Waterford Crystal was sold in more than 50 countries throughout the world. In many, sales were modest but margins still justified a presence provided there was reasonable representation available and limited marketing costs. For example, current sales in Thailand amounted to between £150,000 and £200,000 per annum.

When Waterford committed to a major marketing investment in 1988 it was not surprising that Japan was chosen. It offered several major advantages.

- It was an affluent market with a population in excess of 120 million
- It had a reputation as a very brand conscious market
- Wedgwood already had a significant presence in that market and were in a position to handle distribution.
- Gift giving was a major element of Japanese culture.

None of these factors guaranteed success, however. On the other hand, Japan did not have a large premium crystal market. As in several other countries, the extent of the market was influenced by local cultural factors. In the period from 1988, when Waterford first entered the Japanese market, to the current year, 1995, Waterford had invested £5 million in developing the Japanese market. This figure includes only external promotional costs and takes no account of management time or travelling costs. Returns had been slow and sales were expected to reach close to £2 million in 1995. They were continuing to grow. The slow growth was not aided by the recession which was currently apparent in Japan. However, Waterford was confident that by 1997 it would be showing a satisfactory return on investment with sales in excess of £3 million. Retail prices of both Waterford and Wedgwood were high in Japan partly as a marketing strategy and partly reflecting the enormous power of department stores in the Japanese distribution channel.

Attempts to enter other markets were sporadic and limited in success. Recent focus groups research undertaken in France and Spain indicated that consumers in both countries did not like the cut, feel, weight or price of Waterford Crystal. They had no knowledge of the brand and to cap it all, they liked Marquis even less. Sales in continental Europe were almost non existent rarely amounting to more than £100,000 in any one country. Yet, these were affluent markets. Craftsmen from continental Europe had, twice, in the seventeenth and twentieth centuries inspired the development of cut crystal at Waterford.

WATERFORD CRYSTAL IN THE USA

As previously noted, the US market directly accounted for 75% of all Waterford Crystal sales. Since the product began to develop significant sales in the sixties, Waterford had controlled its own distribution and marketing. It operated from a 250,000 sq. ft distribution and administration centre in the New Jersey. The US subsidiary was Waterford Wedgwood Inc. which reported to Waterford Crystal headquarters in Waterford. It was also responsible for the distribution and marketing of Wedgwood in the US.

In total, the US subsidiary employed 600 staff. Of these 150 were employed directly in almost 30 Waterford Wedgwood stores. Most of these were located in outlet malls, of which there are an estimated 400 throughout the US. These malls typically have a series of prestige branded product outlets in areas such as clothing and gifts and, in many cases, marketed items which were no longer on that brand's top fashion list. These stores accounted for about 12% of Waterford's turnover in the US. They retailed only Waterford and Wedgwood brands with the minor exceptions of some products deemed to be complementary.

Most of the balance of the turnover was through department stores. It had long been the policy of Waterford that its products would be retailed in the best outlet, or outlets, in each city or town. In total, Waterford Wedgwood Inc. had 3000 US accounts though, in many instances, an account might represent several stores. The biggest customer was Federated whose outlets included Bloomingsdales and Macys. Other major prestige outlets included Richs in Atlanta, Burdines in Florida, Marshall Fields in Chicago, Robinson in Los Angeles and Foleys and Nieman Marcus in Texas and neighbouring states. The company takes great care that its products are only available in stores that can display and market the product in a manner that reflects the Waterford image. Waterford and its sister brand Marquis were generally available in the same outlets. As previously noted, Waterford sought to have separate displays for the two ranges. However, in practice, the displays tended to be next to each other or across the aisle from each other.

It was a source of some concern that crystal retailing generally took place on upper floors in a department store. This reflected the relative value of floor space to retailers. Faster moving or more convenience type products tended to be placed on lower floors. For example, Macys retailed crystal, including Waterford, on the 7th floor. Redmond O'Donoghue, who was a frequent visitor to US department stores, had often remarked wryly that customers who suffered from vertigo were unlikely to purchase Waterford Crystal!

Waterford Wedgwood Inc in the US had a major role in new product planning for the whole company. It had its own product planning groups which worked closely with the design unit based at corporate headquarters in Ireland. The product planners also worked closely with key staff in retail outlets and tested new product ideas on consumers. The company also commissioned research on a regular basis and noted closely research carried out by independent organisations which impinged on the company. An example of the former was recent research on consumer reasons for purchasing Waterford. In descending order of importance the following reasons figured prominently

• quality
• design
• "Waterford makes products right for me"
• "Waterford products don't go out of style"
• "Waterford never discontinues a pattern"

The last reason applied only to stemware such as wine glasses. It was Waterford's policy to guarantee to replace or add to any collection of stemware where, for example, a customer had damaged a piece or where a customer wished to increase the number of place settings. The customer, of course, paid for this facility and might have to wait for up to 6 months for a replacement. Such orders were grouped into batches and were put through the factory when an economic lot was assembled. This facility was lightly used but customers indicated, through the research, that they valued its availability. To reinforce this, Waterford had recently arranged a series of instore promotions featuring all stemware suites manufactured since the company was founded. Consumers were encouraged to visit these displays and identify any pieces where they were short of a complete set or wished to add to it.

The same research placed the fact that the products were hand crafted and cut, low on their list of reasons to purchase and the fact that the products were made in Ireland hardly rated at all. The relatively low weighting to the hand crafted feature pointed up an issue for Waterford which has already been discussed.

Other research of note, which had reflected on the Waterford brand, included a major independent research study on 6000 consumers who were invited to rate 500 brands in terms of perceived quality. Waterford rated 8th in this survey behind such brands as Disney, BMW, Mercedes and, perhaps surprisingly, at No. 1, Kodak.

In an earlier study among high income earners Waterford rated second in awareness and esteem. A similar study, by the same organisation, in the UK, placed Waterford in first position. Yet, in other major continental European markets, the brand was virtually unknown.

Promotion of Waterford followed a fairly set pattern. Above the line promotion focused mostly on key major magazines targeted at high earner groups. An average of 200 pages per year were placed. Most other promotion focused on events designed to place Waterford in front of consumers. One such regular event was what was described as an artisan event when craftsmen were brought from Waterford to key US outlets where they showed their craft and signed or otherwise personalised Waterford products. The sports trophy programme was also a major promotional vehicle. Waterford was associated with many major sports events usually through the presentation of a trophy. This part of Waterford's operation was a separate profit centre. However, where the event was highly prestigious, and/or received major coverage in media, the trophy would be specially designed by Waterford and supplied at no cost. Sports supported by Waterford included tennis, golf, horse racing and motor racing. Two examples included the German Formula One Motor Racing Grand Prix at Hockenheim and the major ATP Top 8 tournament, also staged in Germany, at the end of the tennis season.

Waterford was also a major sponsor of the annual Miss America Pageant in Atlantic City in September. The winner is presented with a Waterford Crystal sceptre and Waterford Crystal pays $25,000 to a charity nominated by the winner. The event continues to be one of the three most watched television shows of the year in the US.

A key, largely uncontrollable, factor in Waterford's business in the US was the value of the US dollar against European currencies and, particularly, the Irish pound. The Irish currency was obviously a very small player on world currency markets. Its relationship with the US dollar had fluctuated widely in the past ten years. It ranged from $0.95 to IR£1 at the dollar's high point in the late eighties to $1.80 to £1 in the early nineties. Currently it was trading in the range of $1.50 to $1.60 to £1. It was not possible for a Company such as Waterford Crystal to recover fluctuations of a negative type as the US market was largely insulated from major international currency movements. Where it was likely to influence sales, was in Ireland, to US tourists. A low value of the dollar tended to discourage US visitors and depress their spending power. A high dollar value had the opposite effect. Waterford sought to smooth out currency fluctuations by selling dollars forward. It normally sold dollars at a fixed price for up to two years ahead.

LOOKING AHEAD

As he neared his home in Waterford, Redmond O'Donoghue reflected on how far Waterford Crystal had come in its almost 50 years of existence and the mistakes that had been made along the way. He was conscious that he might look back on this day as a defining moment in his own career. The "Chairman's Challenge" to double both turnover and profit in five years, seemed both daunting and exciting in equal measures. He decided to call an urgent meeting of all key executives available on the following day. While cost reduction would be likely to form a key part of a strategy to double turnover and profit in five years, the strategy would have to be strongly marketing driven. In considering the next day's meeting, he felt that it was important that it should quickly develop a clear strategy focus. There were some good development projects in the pipeline that could go some way to meeting the targets but were unlikely to bring the company anywhere close to the targets which he was now considering. The shape of the next day's meeting would be important as a start in a process that would have to be largely complete within three months.

TEACHING NOTES

Teaching notes for these case studies are available to lecturers. Requests, which must be on college writing paper, should be sent to:

The Marketing Institute
South County Business Park
Leopardstown
Dublin 18
Tel   :   01-295 2355
Fax: :   01-295 2453
Email :   education@mii.ie
Website   www.mii.ie